Elements in Language Teaching
edited by
Heath Rose
University of Oxford
Jim McKinley
University College London

DATA-DRIVEN LEARNING IN AND OUT OF THE LANGUAGE CLASSROOM

Pascual Pérez-Paredes
University of Murcia

Alex Boulton
University of Lorraine

Shaftesbury Road, Cambridge CB2 8EA, United Kingdom

One Liberty Plaza, 20th Floor, New York, NY 10006, USA

477 Williamstown Road, Port Melbourne, VIC 3207, Australia

314–321, 3rd Floor, Plot 3, Splendor Forum, Jasola District Centre,
New Delhi – 110025, India

103 Penang Road, #05–06/07, Visioncrest Commercial, Singapore 238467

Cambridge University Press is part of Cambridge University Press & Assessment,
a department of the University of Cambridge.

We share the University's mission to contribute to society through the pursuit of
education, learning and research at the highest international levels of excellence.

www.cambridge.org
Information on this title: www.cambridge.org/9781009511421

DOI: 10.1017/9781009511384

When citing this work, please include a reference to the DOI 10.1017/9781009511384

First published 2025

A catalogue record for this publication is available from the British Library

ISBN 978-1-009-51142-1 Hardback
ISBN 978-1-009-51143-8 Paperback
ISSN 2632-4415 (online)
ISSN 2632-4407 (print)

Additional resources for this publication at www.cambridge.org/ELAT_Perez-Parades

Data-Driven Learning In and Out of the Language Classroom

Elements in Language Teaching

DOI: 10.1017/9781009511384
First published online: May 2025

Pascual Pérez-Paredes
University of Murcia

Alex Boulton
University of Lorraine

Author for correspondence: Pascual Pérez-Paredes, pascualf@um.es

Abstract: Data-Driven Learning can be broadly defined as the use of corpus tools and techniques for learners and teachers of foreign or second language, typically in the form of concordances derived from authentic texts for inductive learning of lexicogrammar. This Element is a practical guide for language teachers and graduate students intending to explore or upgrade their use of corpora in the language classroom and beyond. In today's context, where advances in computing and information processing dominate our social and professional interactions, the use of corpora emerges as a prime resource with which to approach data-driven language learning and teaching, developing language awareness, noticing skills and critical thinking for learning that generative AI cannot do for you.

This Element also has a video abstract: www.cambridge.org/ELAT-PerezParades

Keywords: Corpora and language teaching, corpus literacy, digital language learning, corpora and language learning, Data-Driven Learning

ISBNs: 9781009511421 (HB), 9781009511438 (PB), 9781009511384 (OC)
ISSNs: 2632-4415 (online), 2632-4407 (print)

Contents

1 What Is Data-Driven Learning?

1.1 Introduction

This Element has been written for language teachers, graduate students, and professionals in Teaching English (or other languages) to Speakers of Other Languages (TESOL), language education and applied linguistics with little or no prior experience in corpus linguistics. We have aimed to keep things simple and accessible, introducing the basics step by step. This Element discusses the use of corpora and other tools to enhance language teaching and learning, highlighting the importance of authentic texts and inductive learning – learning by exploring the language with appropriate tools, as opposed to 'being taught'. The Element has been designed as a practical guide for those wishing to find out more about Data-Driven Learning (DDL). It provides a general overview of the use of corpora in language education as well as more specific discussions about ways to implement DDL across different teaching scenarios.

DDL is an approach to language teaching and learning based on the tools and techniques of corpus linguistics to enhance learners' understanding of how language is used across linguistic genres. A corpus is usually an electronic collection of authentic texts designed to be representative of a language or language variety (e.g. Spanish, or contemporary teenage speech, or research articles in a given scientific discipline). The point of DDL is for foreign or second language (L2) learners to explore how language actually works, as opposed to the traditional 'being taught'. DDL favours inductive learning and general cognitive skills such as critical thinking, pattern detection, hypothesis building, data analysis, and noticing. Thanks to the large and increasing body of research in this area, we know that DDL promotes learner autonomy and language awareness.

A corpus (plural *corpora*) often contains millions or billions words, written or spoken by hundreds or thousands of different people, thus providing an insight into real usage over a wide range rather than the intuitions of a few individuals who may produce coursebooks or other materials. For example, the British National Corpus (BNC)[1] was designed in the late 1980s to represent the English language used in the UK. More recently, the Corpus of Contemporary American English (COCA)[2] was built to illustrate English as used in the United States of America. The former contains 100 million words, the latter 1 billion in 2024, and is still growing. However, not all corpora are this big. Smaller corpora can be useful to study very specific varieties of language use (e.g. research papers in the field of dentistry), or to provide an example of an actual piece of

---

[1] www.english-corpora.org/bnc.
[2] www.english-corpora.org/coca.

research (e.g. the articles published about a celebrity during a period of time in a given newspaper).

Human beings create and shape their understanding of reality through the use of language, which involves engaging in different forms of communication. This can include spoken interactions, such as conversations and speeches; written formats, like books, articles, and social media posts; and hybrid modes, which combine elements of both, such as digital communication that may involve text, audio, or visual content simultaneously. Through these discursive practices, individuals interpret their experiences, share their thoughts, and construct the meanings that define their social and personal realities. Corpora are resources that facilitate the study of how the speakers of a language use it across different linguistic genres such as fiction, news, conversation, TV shows, and academic language. Corpora, in essence, provide evidence of how human beings construct their reality discursively by engaging in spoken, written or hybrid communication modes. Corpora, therefore, have the potential to show how a community of speakers uses language to fulfil real communicative functions, presenting contextualised authentic language usage. Corpora have been used to build dictionaries based on real use of the language, to study the grammar of English, to understand how humans generate discourses based on ideologies or, just to name one other area of application, to attribute authorship in forensic linguistics.

A list of online resources and software for DDL specifically compiled for this Element can be found at https://doi.org/10.48316/DgLhT-C33sa (Pérez-Paredes & Boulton, 2024).

One of the most important uses of corpora is in language education. Before the widespread availability of personal computers, a few teachers in the late 1960s were already making use of printed concordance lines (McEnery & Wilson, 1997) to explore actual language patterns in English for Specific Purposes (ESP). It was this possibility that sparked the interest of these pioneering teachers in what concordance lines could bring to language learning. This is useful to both language teachers and learners, who cannot always find frequency-based evidence of usage in dictionaries or textbooks. We will find some examples of these uses in Sections 3 and 4, where we will discuss the use of corpora in secondary-school contexts and in academic writing teaching contexts, respectively.

In this Element, we will examine language learners' use of and engagement with concordance lines such as those in Figure 1. Each line is a short extract of text from a corpus that shows a word or phrase in its immediate context, and can easily be printed out to create activities. For reasons of space, Figure 1 shows just a few of the hundreds of lines available in the corpus. The focus word or phrase (here *sort of*) remains in the centre of the line, allowing the user to read the words that appear

Figure 1 *sort of* concordance lines from the 2014 Spoken British National Corpus

both to the left and to the right and see how the word or phrase is used in context. These concordance lines are a random selection taken from a pool of 14,437 occurrences of *sort of* in 10.5 million words of spoken English in the 2014 British National Corpus (BNC).[3] Each of those occurrences is an attested, authentic use that can be situated in a specific text and context. Exploring these lines involves detailed, usage-driven observation of the contexts where the phrase appears in spoken language, and the words that usually accompany their use (e.g. *thing, like, stuff, know*).[4] The concordance lines also show that *sort of* in spoken British English is followed by a singular noun in almost 30 per cent of the instances and by a plural noun in only 6 per cent. Adjectives are found after *sort of* in 6 per cent of the attested uses; *–ing* verbs and verbs in the simple past are more frequent than any other verbal forms. Although nowadays concordance lines are always generated by downloadable software or by online platforms (see Section 3), using printed concordance lines in the classroom has been, and continues to be, a standard way to show learners how words are combined in actual usage.

This type of detailed analysis of 'words in context' (lexical items embedded in strings of natural discourse) highlights the frequent patterns of how language is typically used: in other words, we are not dealing with grammar rules that show what is possible, but normal use that shows what is probable. It more closely reflects our current thinking of how language is learned, stored and used (usage-based theories; see e.g. Tomasello, 2003), and the DDL approach has been shown to increase language learners' awareness about the structure of the language, and language teachers' and material developers' sensitivity to the need to incorporate such description of usage in language teaching materials

---

[3] https://cass.lancs.ac.uk/bnc2014.

[4] In linguistics, 'usage' refers to how language is actually used by speakers and writers in real-world contexts, as opposed to how it might be prescribed by formal grammar rules or traditional standards. Studying usage involves observing and describing the patterns, choices, and variations people make when communicating. This includes vocabulary selection, grammar structures, pronunciation, and even stylistic choices, reflecting the dynamic nature of language.

(see Adolphs & Carter, 2003, for an analysis of *like* in conversation and a proposal to incorporate those findings to the *Cambridge Advanced Grammar of English*).

1.2 Data-Driven Learning and the TaLC Community

In DDL, discovering language patterns becomes the quintessential activity for both teachers and learners. Tim Johns coined the term *Data-Driven Learning* in 1990 to describe the type of corpus-driven work that the author himself encouraged in a group of international students in the UK when learning grammar. Some of the questions that came up during his sessions included 'What is the difference between *therefore* and *hence*?' or 'Why aren't all *shoulds* real *shoulds*?' In Johns' words, concordance lines allow the teacher to abandon the role of expert and take on that of a research organiser to help in the discovery of language patterns, embracing the 'I'm not sure: let's find out together' maxim (Johns, 1990, p. 31). To answer this type of question, it was necessary to examine the concordance lines generated by a specific type of software: a concordancer. Four years earlier, Johns (1986) had created *Micro-Concord,* software that allowed language teachers and learners to generate concordance lines on a Spectrum computer. It is fascinating to think that almost 40 years later, we are living the early years of Generative Artificial Intelligence (GenAI) and Large Language Models (LLMs). We will come back to this point in Section 5.

In 1994, the first edition of the Teaching and Language Corpora (TaLC) biennial conference series was held at the Lancaster University in the UK. Since then, it has brought together researchers, lecturers, language teachers and other professionals interested in the use of corpora in language education. TaLC has served as a catalyst for the discussion of teaching practices in DDL, promoting the publication of volumes that feature cutting-edge research and workshops that showcase the latest developments in software, applications and classroom practices. The latest TaLC-inspired volumes (Charles & Frankenberg-Garcia, 2021; Götz & Mukherjee, 2019; Leńko-Szymańska & Boulton, 2015; Pérez-Paredes & Mark, 2021; Tyne & Spina, in press) include discussions about, among other things, language learners' engagement with corpora and corpus tools, the design of DDL activities, and how analyses of learner language can inform teaching practice. TaLC is one of the largest, if not the largest, community of researchers and teachers worldwide that discusses uses of corpora for the teaching of languages across a variety of learning contexts and a great meeting point to discuss the affordances and the challenges behind the use of corpora for language teaching.

There have been thousands of academic publications on DDL over the last 40-plus years, of which at least 800 provide some kind of empirical evaluation.

Because it can be difficult to make sense of such large quantities of research, various researchers have produced a number of syntheses. The broadest to date is Boulton and Vyatkina (2021), which coded 489 papers to examine how the main areas covered have changed over time. They followed this up with a more focused look at DDL for English language teaching, based on papers in highly cited journals (Boulton & Vyatkina, 2024). Pérez-Paredes (2022) explored key clusters from five journals over a five-year period, arguing that DDL needs to become 'normalised' – that is, part of the everyday practice in language classrooms. Dong et al. (2023) used a bibliometric analysis to identify the principal research themes and contributors to the DDL paradigm. Most relevant for present purposes are probably the various meta-analyses that have been carried out, a meta-analysis being a method for combining quantitative results from different studies. Though meta-analyses are not without their drawbacks, they do afford a broader view as they enable the pooling of many studies into a single whole, with each of the included papers featuring data from different types of DDL in different contexts, with different learners, corpora, tools, and procedures. Boulton and Cobb (2017) included sixty-four studies in the field DDL as a whole, finding large effect sizes overall (i.e. DDL is in the top quartile, providing better results than 75 per cent of other meta-analyses in second language acquisition according to Plonsky and Oswald (2014))". Like most meta-analyses, they also divided the sample into groups to explore different 'moderator variables' (e.g. comparing hands-on concordancing and paper-based DDL, or with learners at different levels of proficiency), concluding that 'DDL works pretty well in almost any context' where we have sufficient data (p. 386). Ueno and Takeuchi (2023) followed similar procedures for more recent research, finding medium effect sizes but their methodology is not beyond criticism (see Boulton et al., in press). Lee et al. (2019) focused on DDL for vocabulary, where the twenty-nine studies included showed large effect sizes for learning both referential meanings and syntactic features. Most recently, Ngo and Chen (2024) looked at thirty studies of corpus use in ESL/EFL writing, again with large effect sizes. The conclusion: DDL works, and it works well! But like all studies in language teaching and learning, it varies in how well it works according to any number of factors – the learners' age, proficiency, needs and aims, the tools and corpora used and the activities to accompany them, and so on. DDL has potential; whether it will work for you and your students is something you can only try.

1.3 Linguistic Data and Language Teaching

DDL seeks to foster learners' inductive learning where authentic language data from corpora provide opportunities for discovery and internalisation of usage in an effective way (Boulton & Vyatkina, 2021). This is well reflected in collections of DDL activities such as Viana (2022) or Le Foll (2021), which have brought together classroom resources that aim to provide teachers with ready-to-use activities for exploring formulaic language, collocations and language patterns, among other things. In the following sections, we will examine DDL activities as well as corpora and strategies to use corpora in the classroom.

Researchers in language learning have shown that both explicit and implicit instruction methods have a significant impact on L2 learning, although it seems that implicit instruction shows longer-lasting effects on learning compared to explicit instruction (Kang et al., 2019). While in explicit L2 instruction learners are taught grammar or vocabulary through explanations or drills, implicit language learning involves exposure to language input without overt instruction on grammar rules or language structures. According to the meta-analysis on form-focused instruction carried out by Kang et al. (2019), implicit learning takes place through pattern recognition, incidental learning, repeated exposure to language input and unconscious cognitive processes. DDL is well positioned to favour a wide spectrum of implicit and explicit language learning (O'Keeffe, 2021), encouraging attention to linguistic form. In DDL, language learners examine linguistic evidence in terms of words, word combinations and patterns (Hunston, 2019), and formulate their own hypotheses about how language works, which may lead to the development of language skills and knowledge. This constructivist approach means that learners are deriving their own 'rules' (i.e. formulations of language patterns) from the language they encounter. While their rules may be less accurate than those a teacher could provide (though this is not always the case!), the process requires significant thinking (cognitive depth), and the rules will be meaningful to each individual; for both these reasons, they are more likely to be retained.

In DDL, teachers and learners interact with two types of language data. The first type of data is the corpus itself. A corpus can be conceptualised as a group of texts that have been collected to increase our understanding of how language is used. Understanding the composition of the corpus helps to make sense of the data that can be extracted from the corpus. As McEnery and Brezina (2022) have put it, knowing the purpose of the corpus, the language varieties included, and any biases in the data collection process helps users interpret the linguistic phenomena observed in the analysis. A well-designed corpus can reveal the discursive practices of the speakers of a language, either because the corpus represents the main genres they use (e.g. fiction, blogs, and conversation), or because the corpus focuses on one specific genre across time.

The second type of linguistic data in DDL is the insights gained by examining a corpus. These insights fall within one of the following four categories: frequency measures, collocations, language patterning, and genre awareness

(Pérez-Paredes, 2022). Table 1 offers a summary of what these insights mean for language teachers and learners.

More broadly, Boulton and Cobb (2017, pp. 350–351) argue that DDL aligns with current theories in a number of fields:

- Linguistics: rather than being rule-based, language is probabilistic, dynamic and complex, interactive and patterned; knowledge is based on an amalgam of all previous encounters.
- Learning: rules are hard because they are an 'artificial intellectual abstraction', while patterns are easier, reflecting an innate ability to make sense of the complex world around us.
- Psycholinguistics: while pattern detection involves deep cognitive processing, the naturalness of it reduces cognitive load, thus freeing up space for attention to meaning.

Table 1 Insights from corpus data consultation and analysis

Frequency measures	Frequency information can help language learners and teachers prioritise which words and phrases to focus on for vocabulary acquisition. High-frequency items are more likely to be encountered in real-world communication and are essential for building a solid language foundation (Szudarski, 2022).
Collocations	Words occur together in natural language in non-random ways. Learning and using collocations can make learners' L2 more natural and idiomatic, contributing to fluency (Friginal & Roberts, 2022).
Language patterning	Awareness of language patterns enables language learners to communicate more effectively and fluently. If learners understand and use language patterns to convey meaning accurately, they are more likely to produce language that sounds natural (Gablasova & Bottini, 2022).
Genre awareness	Corpus data and frequency analysis allows teachers and learners to identify variations in language use across genres (e.g. business emails or lab reports) or language varieties (e.g. Spanish in Mexico or Spain). Frequency information across genres provides insights into what is preferred by the users of different genres and facilitates our understanding of how vocabulary and patterning work in a given genre.

- Second language acquisition: effective learning requires a balance between top-down processing (meaning in discourse and context) and bottom-up (from sounds, words or grammar to create meaning), with language at the centre of communication.

DDL also reflects existing learner practices, involving aspects of computers that learners are already familiar with and doing in their own time (searching for answers to their questions and interpreting the results they find on the internet). In fact, various authors have attributed all kinds of attributes to DDL, such as authenticity, autonomy, communication, consciousness-raising, constructivism, context, critical thinking, discovery learning, dynamic systems theory, focus on form, heuristics, Information and Communication Technology (ICT), individualisation, induction, input flood, languaging, learner-centeredness, learning-to-learn, life-long learning, Languages for Specific Purposes (LSP), (meta-)cognition, meaningfulness, mobile learning, motivation, needs, noticing, responsibility, salience, scaffolding, sensitisation, strategy training, styles and preferences, tasks, transferability, and so on. We will not develop all these here: suffice to say that there are numerous reasons to think that DDL has much to contribute to L2 learning and use.

1.4 DDL in the 2020s and Beyond

DDL practices have undergone considerable changes in the last two decades. These changes have affected the types of resources for DDL as well as the scope of classroom practices. One of the most visible is a shift from small corpora of up to 1 million words to corpora of billions of words. There have also been shifts from desktop-software-only applications to web corpus management tools that facilitate access anywhere, any time; from workstations and labs for hands-on learning to students' use of their own personal devices, including tablets. Additionally, there has been a continuous interest in expanding DDL to other languages and other curricula, including secondary education and professional situations. In essence, DDL has become more open to a wider range of teaching contexts, languages, and tools.

One of the areas where DDL has undergone change is the use of a variety of resources in language classrooms, not just corpora. As we will discuss in Section 3, DDL has made use of texts and collections of texts that were not meant to represent language varieties or to support linguistic research. Such collections tend to be smaller and to show some flexibility in terms of their composition. Classroom resources do not necessarily make use of corpora that are representative of a language or variety, but of the type of language which is needed by language learners. Such observations prompted the idea of Broad

Data-Driven Language (BDDL). BDDL (Pérez-Paredes, 2024) can be implemented more straightforwardly in classrooms as the corpus resources are either typically put together by teachers, which makes them in principle more readily accessible to learners or are simply available on the internet. Such resources include, among many others, collocation dictionaries, collocation tools, phrase extraction tools, grammar pattern identification tools, and n-gram generators.[5] This list highlights some important concepts in corpus linguistics. First, collocates are words that occur together more often than you would expect by chance. One example is *blond* which typically collocates with very few items in English – *hair* (including *curls*, *beard*, etc.) or *people* with such hair (*woman*, *child*, etc.). This may seem obvious, but such patterns of usage are not identical between languages: customers frequently ask for *une bière blonde* in French, where English would prefer another term such as *lager* over *blond beer*. The concept of *phrase* needs little explanation, but corpus linguistics has no notion of meaningful groups. What it can do however is to detect *n-grams*, which is a sequence of *n* items (usually words), regardless of whether they constitute a meaningful unit (See Section 2). So *one of* is a 2-gram (or bigram), *one of the* is a 3-gram, *one of the most* is a 4-gram, *one of the most important* is a 5-gram, *one of the most important things* is a 6-gram, and so on.[6] Different people use different labels for these groups (e.g., clusters or chunks), but the point is that they show the patterns in language and how they can be built up, broken down, and where variation is more or less likely.

BDDL enhances language learners' engagement with language, facilitating their analysis of linguistic patterns and structures, and identification of recurring word combinations or collocations. The interpretation of language data is essential for extracting meaningful information from corpora and other language-driven sources, and for applying it to language learning. This is, in our view, a core feature of data/corpus literacy that will be essential in new ecologies of digital language learning that have already emerged (Gee & Hayes, 2011) and which are likely to be shaken by the impact of LLMs on language learning. In Section 3, we will discuss in detail how corpora and GenAI afford data analysis and language learning.

In a context where natural language processing technologies and GenAI evolve rapidly and where we can expect massive changes in the way we interact with computers, interpreting language data for language learning is a core component of new digital literacies via GenAI. Working with corpora and

---

[5] A list of resources for English can be found on www.perezparedes.es/selected-corpus-resources-for-second-language-educators.

[6] *One of* is among the most frequent 2 grams in COCA, which is most frequently followed by *the* and then the other words in each of the examples given.

using DDL activities can help our students reframe how language data is generated and presented, and how it can be interpreted in language education. In this context, learners will have to:

- Understand data concepts. These include types of data, structured (e.g. a table with headings and/or variable names) vs. unstructured datasets (e.g. running text), data sources, and data formats.
- Interpret data. This involves frequency and its impact on language use, including basic understanding of charts and tables and drawing conclusions from data visualisations.
- Analyse data. This draws on basic concepts from corpus linguistics (cf. the 20 basic Corpus Linguistics skills in Pérez-Paredes, 2020).
- Communicate data. Talking about language data can help students process frequency-based information and can help teachers scaffold activities that can enhance their understanding of how learners can infer language properties from the data presented in corpus consultation or other soft DDL tools discussed above.

1.5 This Element

The initial challenges of DDL for beginners, such as preparing corpora and using tools, can feel intimidating. Addressing these obstacles could further ease practitioners into DDL. Our overall aim is to equip language teachers and graduate students in TESOL, applied linguistics and language education programs with skills to promote language awareness and critical thinking in their students. The Element has been structured to facilitate the progressive acquisition of knowledge about DDL and the use of corpora in language teaching. Sections 2 to 5 each emphasise distinct themes, but many of these can be useful in other areas; for example, the discussion about using DDL with young learners in Section 3 leads to an examination of the different roles that language teachers may adopt when using corpora; similarly, the discussion of spoken data or learner corpora in Section 5 is potentially relevant in other situations. The reader is encouraged to tailor their reading experience according to individual preferences. The structure of the Element features six sections including this one. The next section covers the essentials, while Sections 3, 4, and 5 each introduce specific scenarios:

- **Section 2** surveys various existing corpora and their applications in DDL. It outlines different DDL activities and the use of concordancers – tools that help analyse language patterns found in the texts. The section also discusses the basics of querying corpora in the classroom, providing teachers with practical insights into how to effectively integrate these resources into their teaching practices. It emphasises the importance of hands-on DDL and the need for teachers to be well prepared.

- **Section 3** examines the use of corpora to develop relevant DDL resources for younger students. It outlines strategies for creating pedagogic corpora tailored to educational needs, emphasising the selection of learner-relevant data. The section provides real-world examples of how young learners can use language data effectively in classroom settings. The two scenarios show that through hands-on engagement with pedagogically relevant texts, students can be immersed in activities that favour language acquisition, highlighting the practical benefits of DDL in enhancing learning outcomes.

- **Section 4** explores the potential of DDL in university settings, particularly in teaching academic writing. It demonstrates how corpora can support language use for both general and specific academic purposes, showing how students can benefit from analysing research articles and other academic texts. The section presents scenarios that illustrate effective DDL practices in higher education, emphasising the skills necessary to engage learners critically with academic language and improve their writing proficiency.

- **Section 5** expands upon the idea of learner autonomy, emphasising the versatility and adaptability of DDL methods in and beyond DDL. The scenarios here can go beyond conventional classroom environments, enabling learners to interact with language data on their own, cultivating a sense of ownership on their educational journey. By leveraging accessible resources and technology, it demonstrates how DDL can empower students to take control of their learning process.

- **Section 6** recaps the main ideas discussed in the Element, offering insights about the future of DDL.

1.6 Summary and Take-Home Message

This section has presented DDL as a teaching approach that leverages corpora to improve language education. We have discussed the significance of using authentic language and promoting inductive learning, which nurtures critical thinking and language awareness in language learners. The section has also explored the function of common general corpora for DDL. Understanding how to use language data and collections of texts is crucial for learning languages in a digital world (Gee & Hayes, 2011). This is especially true with the changes that large language models (LLMs) are bringing to computer-human being interfaces and to language learning.

2 A Brief Survey of Existing Corpora and Applications

2.1 Introduction

The increasing interest in recent decades for what corpora can offer to language learners and teachers has been proportionate to the development of corpus linguistics as a discipline and, to a lesser extent, technology-enhanced language teaching practices. As McCarthy et al. (2021) put it, when language learners examine concordance lines they are asked to relearn how to read text in the sense that reading concordances involves sometimes looking at the centre of each line – the search term or 'node' – and sometimes reading backwards from the right to the left, sometimes forwards to the right, and often reading vertically, with the first word(s) to the right on each line, etc. This is something that most learners will find thought-provoking and hopefully stimulating if they have never worked with a corpus or concordance lines before.

2.2 DDL Activities

So, what types of DDL activities can language teachers use with their students? What do they look like? As we will see in Section 3, language teachers play a crucial role in effective DDL, facilitating the integration of corpus data into regular language teaching, providing their students with guidance in their exploration of language patterns. In other words, successful DDL considers the learners' needs and their curriculum. Despite the need for context-sensitive DDL, there are, fortunately, resources that can inform and guide teachers in their selection of activities. A recent resource book for English teaching using corpora (Viana, 2022) has put together a collection of ready-to-use activities showcasing a wide range of DDL activities for teaching English.[7] Table 2 shows a selection of such activities, target levels and tools, in order to provide a taste of what can be done with a corpus in the English language classroom. They can be used 'as is' or inspire teachers to adapt them to their own contexts (or indeed to other languages), or even to design their own original activities.

The activities in Table 2 offer a panoramic (yet inevitably limited) view of the diversity of foci in DDL. All of them are hands-on activities that involve

---

[7] Elen Le Foll (2021) has put together an open educational book which contains a selection of DDL activities and resources on https://elenlefoll.pressbooks.com/.

Table 2 A selection of DDL activities for the teaching of general English (based on Viana, 2022)

Activity focus	Target students	Resources
• *–ing* vs. *–ed* participial adjectives (e.g. *boring/bored*) • Students identify subjects, modifiers and verbs in concordance lines pp. 33–35	Elementary	British National Corpus www.english-corpora .org/bnc
• Telling the difference between false friends and true cognates • Students search for collocations of target adjectives such as *sensible* pp. 44–48	Elementary & above	British National Corpus www.english-corpora.org/bnc
• Identifying correct and incorrect verb + preposition and adjective + preposition combinations pp. 58–61	Elementary & above	Google Books Ngram Viewer https://books .google.com/ngrams
• Identifying adjective collocates when talking about the weather (e.g. *nice, perfect, pleasant, severe, extreme*) pp. 73–77	Intermediate	Sketch Engine for Language Learning (SKELL) https://skell .sketchengine.eu
• Identifying abstract nouns such as *fact, importance* or *aim* and their verb collocates (e.g. *highlight* or *emphasise*) – this activity is useful in tasks that require the description of pictures such as found in many spoken language exams pp. 122–126	Upper intermediate	Sketch Engine for Language Learning (SKELL) https://skell .sketchengine.eu
• Exploring the use of the noun *gender* in news stories across the world • Students select different collocations and report on their spread (e.g. *gender equality, gender identity, gender gap,* and *gender inequality*) pp. 158–162	Upper intermediate	News on the Web (NOW) Corpus www .english-corpora.org/ now

Table 2 (cont.)

Activity focus	Target students	Resources
• Students extract keywords[8] from amateur online film reviews of their choice pp. 166–170	Advanced	Students choose their own texts to explore https://lextutor.ca/key
• Examination of useful phrases to express opinions, persuade and present arguments • Students brainstorm arguments for and against using mobile phones in the language classroom • Students examine authentic debates and discussions from the European Parliament in order to learn new phrases in context	Advanced	InterCorp European Parliament Corpus https://korpus.cz/ kontext

Note: The page numbers show where these activities can be found in Viana (2022).

students' direct engagement with corpus tools and data to analyse language patterns, collocations, and, in general, usage in context. Hands-off DDL activities, on the other hand, involve tasks where learners interact with data that has previously been selected and analysed by the teacher, often in the form of printed handouts, along with guidance on how to use corpus resources without direct manipulation of the tools. In general, DDL activities seek to favour, among others, the following areas:

- Exploration of contexts of use of specific words or phrases in concordance lines.
- Error analysis in learner writing.
- Vocabulary expansion.
- Grammar exploration.
- Comparative analysis of patterns and vocabulary across different genres.
- Language awareness about formulaic language units such as collocations or n-grams.

---

[8] See Section 4.4.1 for a discussion on the use of keywords.

DDL activities are valuable for their ability to provide language learners with authentic language input, increase language awareness, promote individualised and autonomous learning, and, more generally, improve language-learning skills. In the following sections, we discuss some of the best-known concordancers as well as some of the most-widely used corpora in DDL.

2.3 Concordancers

There are two major types of concordancing software: downloadable desktop concordancers and online concordancers. Desktop concordancers can usually be downloaded from the internet and need to be installed on a personal computer, whether this is a desktop computer or a laptop. This means they are stable and can be used even without an internet connection, and some features can be personalised but, to the best of our knowledge, most are not compatible with tablets, still less smartphones. Online concordancers, on the other hand, can be queried using an internet browser, such as Chrome, Safari, or Firefox, which is an attractive option for those teachers and students who do not want to depend on a specific computer or workstation and need to access their data anywhere. They can potentially be queried using a tablet or a mobile phone, but do depend on an internet connection, and may be updated from time to time.

The most widely used desktop software in the DDL community is AntConc,[9] created and maintained by Laurence Anthony at the University of Waseda, Japan. AntConc is a free tool for language concordancing that gets regular updates and online support. It can be used on any computer with a Windows, Linux, or Mac operating system.[10] The latest version offers the option to use a GenAI account such as ChatGPT, so the user can write their question in 'natural' language rather than having to adapt to an interface; however, this function is not to query the corpus data itself, but to find patterns in the results. For reasons of space, we cannot provide here a comprehensive tutorial covering every aspect of the software. However, a useful YouTube playlist created by Laurence Anthony offers easy-to-follow how-to tutorials (Figure 2) for the

---

[9] www.laurenceanthony.net/software/antconc/. The manual for version 4.3.0 can obtained here: www.laurenceanthony.net/software/antconc/releases/AntConc430/help.pdf.

[10] Laurence Anthony's website offers other corpus-related tools that can be downloaded and used for free. They include, among many others, tools for POS tagging (TagAnt), for the compilation and analysis of open access research articles (AntCorGen), for the annotation and analysis of text structure (AntMover), for converting pdfs to txt (AntFileConverter), and for assessing the vocabulary level and complexity of texts (AntWordProfiler). They can be found on www.laurenceanthony.net/software.

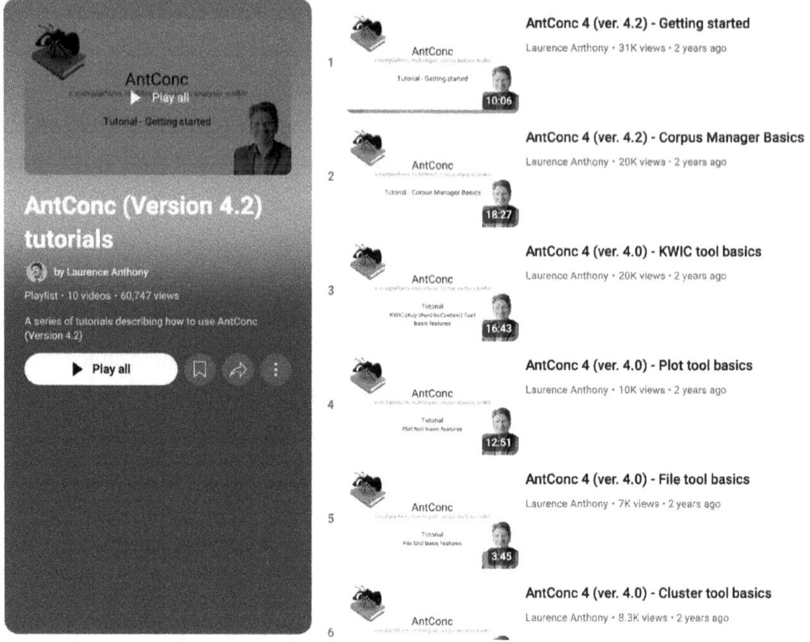

Figure 2 Laurence Anthony's AntConc YouTube tutorials

mechanical aspects.[11] Section 4 offers an overview of how AntConc can be used to teach academic language.

AntConc has been widely used in DDL, not least because Anthony (2024) has always had language learners and teachers in mind, as much as researchers and linguists. Users can upload their own corpora in almost any language, including with other alphabets or characters and right-to-left scripts (e.g. Japanese or Arabic). The corpora are stored on the local hard drive, guaranteeing that the texts remain private and are not uploaded to external servers. One of the unique features in AntConc is that it automatically sorts by patterns – by default, the most frequent word(s) on the right of the search term. The most frequent patterns appear at the top of the list, which makes them more prominent, and the sort options can of course be changed (e.g. to sort to the left). Figure 3 shows examples from a pre-loaded corpus.[12] In AntConc, concordance lines are obtained through the Key Word in Context tab (KWIC: #1 in Figure 3). For example, if we search for *usual*, we can sort the concordance lines using a variety of criteria (#2 in Figure 3). The results

---

[11] www.youtube.com/@AntLabJPN.

[12] BE06: One million words of British English written texts designed to capture a wide range of genres in the mid 2000s – newspapers, fiction, magazines, academic writing, non-fiction, etc. See Baker (2009).

Figure 3 Examining concordance lines using the KWIC tool in AntConc

show the first word to the left (*the*) and the frequency of the occurrences in the selected corpus (*in the usual, of the usual, all the usual*, etc.). The combination of these two deceptively simple features facilitates the identification of language patterns where *usual* is involved (#3 in Figure 3).

Some of the conclusions we can draw from this search include the following:

- When preceded by the definite article and the preposition *in*, we find strings like *in the usual way* or *in the usual location*.
- The use of *usual* is frequent in comparisons and clause-final position: *more than usual, more + ADJECTIVE + than + usual*.
- The use of a possessive determiner before *usual* is very frequent, often followed by a noun that suggests a negative evaluation of someone (*his usual arrogant demeanour, his usual combinations of awkwardness, her usual protest, my usual tactics*).

The above is just a small sample of the contexts that can be explored with AntConc. These results are not exhaustive in any way when dealing with the local grammar of *usual*. As in any corpus exploration, the results can only be tentatively expanded beyond the textual representation provided by the texts and textual genres that make up the corpus being analysed. We return to AntConc in more detail in Section 4.

#LancsBox X (Brezina & Platt, 2024) is another desktop multiplatform program that is particularly strong for data visualisation. As with AntConc, the corpus data remains on a local hard drive although it uses several online services for the part of speech (POS) tagging[13] of the data.[14] #LancsBox X comes with both 2014 and 1994 editions of the British National Corpus (BNC), along with the Lancaster Corpus of Mandarin Chinese, which provides language learners the opportunity to explore widely used corpora for the teaching of the two languages, and others can be uploaded.

Sketch Engine (Kilgarriff et al., 2014) is an online corpus manager that can be accessed from any browser with an internet connection.[15] Although the full version of Sketch Engine is not free, many education institutions provide access to affiliated users, and a more limited version called SkELL (Sketch Engine for Language Learning) is free for several languages. As the name suggests, the limitations of SkELL can be seen as positive for DDL. In particular, there are only three tools: examples (concordances); word sketches (which show items in different grammatical relations to the word queried); and similar words (i.e. synonyms). Further, the examples are not truncated KWIC concordances but full sentences, which can be helpful on first encounter; and the examples given reflect 'good dictionary examples' (GDEX) in that the contexts are not too long nor too short, not too complex nor too simple, and so on.

The full Sketch Engine offers a wide range of ready-to-use corpora in many languages, including the EnTenTen family of corpora: the English Web EnTenTen 2021, for example, is a 52 billion-word corpus made up of texts in English from the internet. A query of the adjective *interesting*, one of the target language points in Table 2, returns over 7 million results − far too many occurrences to look through one by one. Sketch Engine can, however, help users with an automated collocation analysis of all of these concordance lines (Figure 4). Such analysis can give language teachers and learners a comprehensive understanding of the contexts and syntactic functions where this adjective is found. Figure 4 shows the words that pre-modify *interesting* and those that are pre-modified by it. Understanding these contexts of use contributes to enhancing the language learners' understanding of formulaic language. Corpora provide empirical evidence of how *interesting* is used, its distribution and its variability. By analysing corpus data, language teachers and learners can gain valuable insights into the nature and functions of formulaic language in real contexts such as those shown.

---

[13] POS tagging identifies the word class (e.g. noun, adjective, determiner, type of verb, etc.) of every word in the corpus and provides a tag that is stored as part of the corpus and which can be queried.

[14] Video tutorials and the manual are available at: https://lancsbox.lancs.ac.uk.

[15] www.sketchengine.eu.

Figure 4 Some collocations of *interesting* in the EnTenTen21 corpus of English

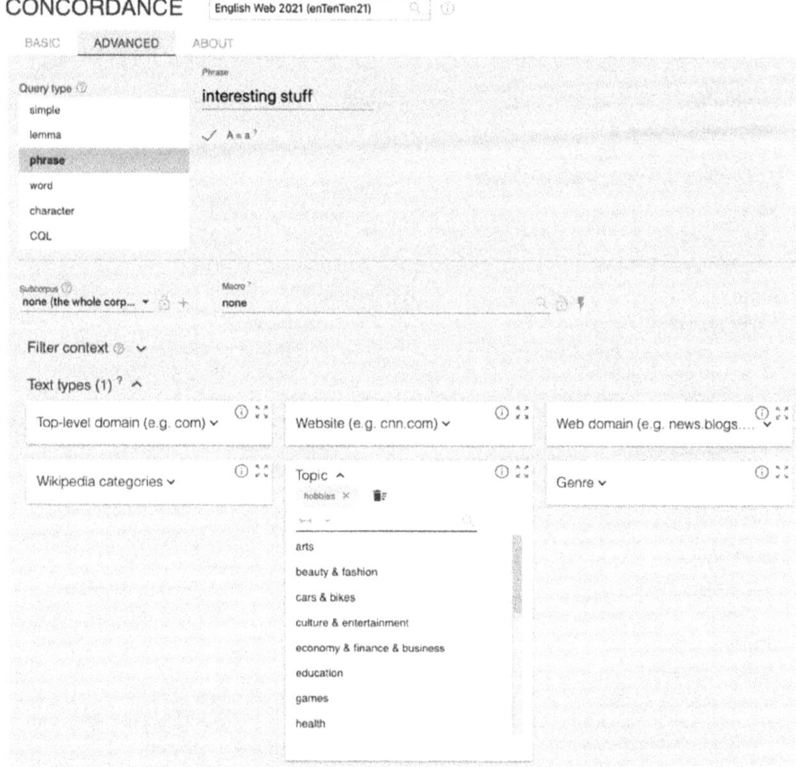

Figure 5 Searching for phrases in a specific topic on Sketch Engine

As can be seen in Figure 4, the Sketch Engine collocation profile shows the domains where a phrase is particularly common. For example, *interesting stuff* is particularly frequent in texts that discuss hobbies. This may seem like a good starting point to link the collocation *interesting + stuff* with the domain where their co-occurrence is particularly frequent, thus providing clues to understanding the use of such a collocation in a broader context. Figure 5 shows how users can narrow down their search and select the topic or topics that may suit them better.

Other features that make Sketch Engine so useful for learning are the possibility to share corpora with other users, or to generate visualisations that represent lexical collocation relations such as those shown in Figure 6, which can be appealing to learners and complement concordance lines or frequency tables.

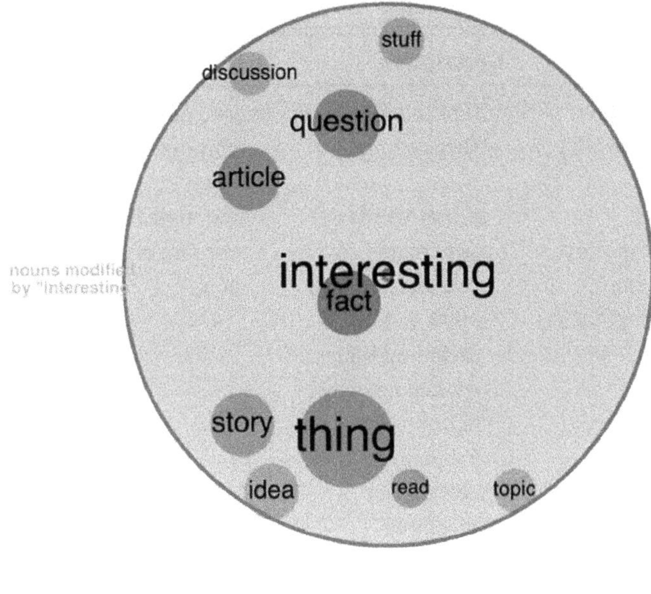

Figure 6 Visualising *interesting* + NOUN collocations in Sketch Engine

2.4 Corpora

When analysing the type of corpus we can use for language teaching, we can look at least at two criteria. First, the availability of the corpus, which can be either restricted access or full access. An all-access corpus gives teachers and learners the possibility to manipulate the files that make up the corpus, add annotation, and use it in the various types of concordance software discussed above. In contrast, a restricted access corpus provides an online search interface through a web browser; this is the case, for example, with all the corpora offered on the www.english-corpora.org website. Table 3 shows a selection of corpora, all regularly used in DDL and of potential interest for English language teaching.

Many of these corpora are widely used in English language teaching (Boulton & Vyatkina, 2024; Pérez-Paredes, 2022). There are other online tools that are of interest to language teachers and learners; most do not allow users to upload their own data, but they do offer easy-to-use interfaces designed to facilitate searching and retrieving results for further analysis. Here we offer a selection:

Table 3 A selection of corpora for language teaching

Corpus	Description	URL	Access
British National Corpus (BNC)	100 million word of British English	www.english-corpora.org/bnc	Restricted
Corpus of Contemporary American English (COCA)	1 billion words of American English between 1999 and 2019 including blogs, spoken language, fiction, magazines, newspaper, academic	www.english-corpora.org/coca	Restricted
TV corpus	325 million words of TV shows recorded in different English-speaking countries from the 1950s and later	www.english-corpora.org/tv	Restricted
News on the Web corpus	19 billion words from web-based newspapers and magazines from 2010 to the present time	www.english-corpora.org/now	Restricted
Sketch Engine for Language Learning (SKELL)	A simplified interface of Sketch Engine adapted to the needs of learners of languages (not only English)	https://skell.sketchengine.eu	Restricted
Corpus of Contemporary American English	English-corpora.org corpora available for download	www.english-corpora.org/coca	All-access Pay license

Table 3 (cont.)

Corpus	Description	URL	Access
(COCA), TV corpus and other english-corpora .org corpora			
British Academic Spoken English Corpus	Lectures and seminars across a range of disciplines	https://ota.bod leian.ox.ac .uk/reposi tory/xmlui/ handle/ 20.500.120 24/2525	All-access
Brown corpus	1 million words of American English texts printed in 1961	www.kaggle .com/data sets/ nltkdata/ brown- corpus	All-access
Movie Scripts Corpus	Almost 3000 movie script texts and annotations by structural elements	www.kaggle .com/data sets/gufu kuro/movie- scripts- corpus	All-access

- CorpusMate.[16] An online tool (Crosthwaite & Baisa, 2024) that provides easy search options of different corpora including:

  o The British Academic Corpus of Written English (BAWE)
  o The British Academic Corpus of Spoken English (BASE)
  o TED Talks Corpus: transcripts of TED talks
  o Simple English Wikipedia
  o BBC Teach: transcriptions of learning videos from BBC Teach website
  o Elsevier OA CC-BY Corpus: a collection of 40,000 scientific articles from across Elsevier's journals.

The results are displayed in different colours to facilitate pattern detection and can be seen in KWIC and sentence formats.

---

[16] https://corpusmate.com/info.

- Linggle.[17] An online site (Lai et al., 2022) designed to provide examples of collocations for learners of English. The search tool is intuitive and suggests patterns (e.g. *provide* NOUN *with* NOUN). Among others, the results are extracted from Google Books.
- Compleat Lexical Tutor.[18] A pioneering suite of tools designed with DDL in mind (Cobb, 2024). It is impossible to offer a summary of the many tools that can be found on this site, including vocabulary profilers, word lists, word frequency identification, frequency-band-informed cloze generators and many more. Users can paste in their own texts.

In many contexts, however, language teachers prefer to build their own corpus. We treat this in depth in Sections 3 and 4. Some potential target corpora can be found these days in Machine Learning dataset repositories.[19] All-access corpora are difficult to come by and these datasets can be of interest if the genres represented in them are something that language teachers want to explore. Some of the genres in the above-mentioned repositories include product reviews, film reviews, fiction, TV scripts, spam SMS texts and emails, news, patent grants, Wikipedia texts or political speeches. There is no one single type of 'best' corpus – it all depends on needs and interests.

2.5 Querying Corpora in the Language Classroom: The Basics

As seen in the previous section, hands-on DDL brings corpora and concordance software to the language classroom. In hands-on DDL, language learners are expected to query a corpus to extract examples of real usage that can help them hypothesise about language patterns. This process is not, however, free from challenges. Corpus consultation involves two distinct stages: the actual search and the interpretation of the search results. Both are equally important and deserve our attention. In general terms, the two stages require some contextual understanding of the context where a word or phrase appears. An actual search usually starts either with a focused word such as *usual* in Figure 3, or a pattern such as VERB + PREPOSITION in Table 2. The search is crucial as it will determine the number and format of concordance lines that will need to be factored in as language learners will examine the surrounding co-text to interpret the meaning of the potential language patterns observed. This interpretation involves the analysis of language features such as syntactic functions and combinatory features (e.g. a NOUN + NOUN sequence suggests that one of the nouns pre-modifies the headword of a noun

---

[17] https://search.linggle.com.   [18] www.lextutor.ca.
[19] For example, www.kaggle.com or https://paperswithcode.com/datasets.

phrase). Learners will be asked to make inferences based on the language evidence in the concordance lines.

Many pedagogical sequences have been proposed for DDL, among the simplest being hypothesis formulation and hypothesis testing (Johns, 2002). More elaborate is the "three 'I's" (Carter & McCarthy, 1995), expanded to include a "fourth I" as an optional third stage (Flowerdew, 2009). This gives us illustration, interaction, (intervention) and induction. These four stages correspond to (i) examining real data, (ii) discussing them with others, (iii) teacher guidance, and (iv) formulating a description. Prior to that of course, the user needs to have a question and formulate it in appropriate way. Perhaps the most complete guidelines for this were formulated by John Sinclair, a British linguist who established the foundations for the use of corpora for modern linguistic research (1991). Among other projects, he was the driving force behind the COBUILD dictionary, the first major dictionary based on the analysis of a corpus of the English language. Sinclair established a methodology to conduct research using corpus data. A clear outline of this methodology can be found in his 2003 book *Reading concordances*. The method outlined there breaks down the steps which are essential to uncover linguistic patterns in a corpus from a linguist's (or learner's) perspective. These steps allow for a rigorous analysis of the corpus data and warrant the hypothesis testing nature of the method. Table 4 shows the main steps involved in interpreting concordance output in this approach.

Of course, a concordance is not the only type of data we can extract from a corpus, but the procedure illustrates how care should be taken in all interpretation. For example, if a word or phrase exists in a corpus, is it frequent enough to be worth learning, and how frequent is it compared to other similar items? Or, if two words collocate, how strong is their relationship, and does it change the meaning of the component items?

In essence, the corpus query process involves searching for lexical items in the corpora and interpreting them in the co-texts that come up in the form of concordance lines. The seven steps outlined below involve analytical work that requires (1) observation of the chosen node and the words to the left and right of it, as well as (2) the formulation of hypotheses about the link between the patterns detected and the meanings we can associate with them. One of the best examples of the work exemplified above is the English grammar patterns that were published as a complement to the English COBUILD Dictionary (Hunston & Francis, 2000). Such grammar patterns were noted by members of the COBUILD research team following the method displayed in Table 4. This is a useful resource for English language teachers that can be accessed online on the Collins Dictionary link.[20] As

---

[20] https://grammar.collinsdictionary.com/grammar-pattern.

Table 4 Corpus query steps according to Sinclair (2003, pp. xxvi–xxviii)

Step	Detailed activities involved
Step 1: Initiate	• Search for a word or a string of words and obtain a set of concordance lines. • Check out the words to the right of the node. Are there words that are repeated in several lines? • Check out the words to the left of the node. Are there words that are repeated in several lines? • Can you find any patterns? The answer to this question is largely a matter of interpretation. For Sinclair, if a word form is found in the same position in more than half the concordance lines, then we could be dealing with a dominant pattern. If what stands out is a word class such as a noun or an adjective, then this can be of interest as well. A combination of a node plus a noun or a preposition, just to cite two different word classes, may suggest a preference for such word class.
Step 2: Interpret	• Examine again the repeated words to the left and to the right of the node. • Come up with a hypothesis that may link all of them or, at least, most of them. Are they from the same word class? Do they all have similar meanings?
Step 3: Consolidate	• Look for other evidence that can support the hypothesis in Step 2. • Find single occurrences that come close to the criterion that you have set up. • Find other structures that express a similar meaning. • Look beyond the word position that you have started with, for example Node + 1 word to the right. Look at more distant words (Node + 3, 4, or 5 to the left or the right). • Revise and loosen up the hypothesis a little if you can include several more instances.
Step 4: Report	• After step 3, write your hypothesis. This way you can always test your insights in the future.
Step 5: Recycle	• Is there another important pattern in the vicinity of the node? Go through steps 1–4 and continue until there are no repeated patterns left. • Examine the instances that have not been included in any of the observed patterns. Are they unusual? In which way?

Table 4 (cont.)

Step	Detailed activities involved
Step 6: Result	• List the hypothesis or hypotheses and link them in a final report on the node.
Step 7: Repeat	• Test your hypothesis on new data from the corpus. Follow the same steps. Confirm or revise the hypotheses as you examine new data.

an example, take the *NOUN* + *against* + *NOUN* pattern in Table 5, inspired by the initial steps in Table 4.

Drawing attention to the use of these patterns in the classroom can become an opportunity to deepen the use of formulaic language in different genres and subjects or domains. Using a large corpus can give learners the opportunity to explore further the combinatory features of some of the above instantiations such as *policy against*. Figure 7 shows some of the collocations (e.g. *zero-tolerance policy against*; *scorched-earth policy against*) that occur significantly often in the corpus data.

The studies on grammar patterns for English are unparalleled in other languages, which may explain why DDL in Languages Other Than English (LOTEs) needs more attention (Pérez-Paredes & Chambers, 2025 in press). However, the availability of very large corpora like Sketch Engine TenTen family[21] in many languages provides opportunities for educators and learners to explore usage across a variety of contexts in LOTEs.

2.6 Hands-on DDL: What Teachers Need to Know

This section draws on Boulton and Pérez-Paredes (2024), which in turn is inspired by decades of DDL research and exploration. Before trying hands-on concordancing, many teachers prefer to begin with printed concordances or other corpus data; this has the advantage of keeping things within the teacher's control, with pre-planned questions and known outcomes, guiding the learners step by step, limiting the possibilities for distraction in large quantities of data, and avoiding technical issues.

• Keep it simple

If you are a language teacher, do not expect your learners to be experts in corpus consultation straightaway. Start with tools that students are familiar

---

[21] www.sketchengine.eu/documentation/tenten-corpora.

Table 5 *Noun +* ***against*** *+ Noun* **pattern**

Step	Detailed activities involved
Step 1: Initiate	• Nouns are usually followed by prepositions such as *against*. • Concordance lines of NOUN + *against* are examined. To do this, for example, a search on Sketch Engine operationalised as [tag="N.*"][word="against"] will return all nouns followed by *against* in the corpus. An introduction to searches can be found in Pérez-Paredes (2020). • Can a pattern be found?

Steps 2–7: Interpret and consolidate	• The hypothesis is that there are different patterns.
	• As a result of applying steps 2–7, different meanings emerge that can be grouped as follows:
	    ○ The *attack* group
	    ○ The *broadside* group
	    ○ The *protection* group
	    ○ The *charge* group
	    ○ The *anger* group
	    ○ The *argument* group
	    ○ The *game* group
	For example, in the *attack* group we find nouns that refer to fighting, opposing someone or something or attempting to harm somebody. The nouns involved are *action, agitation, alliance, assault, attack, backlash, battle, blow, campaign, conspiracy, coup, crime, crusade, demonstration, drive, fight, measure, offence, offensive, onslaught, petition, plot, policy, protest, raid, reaction, rebellion, resistance, revenge, revolt, revolution,* stand, *strike, struggle, uprising, vendetta, violence, vote, war,* and *witch-hunt.*
	The nouns in the *argument* group refer to arguments or evidence. In this group, we find *argument, case, defence,* and *evidence.* And so on.

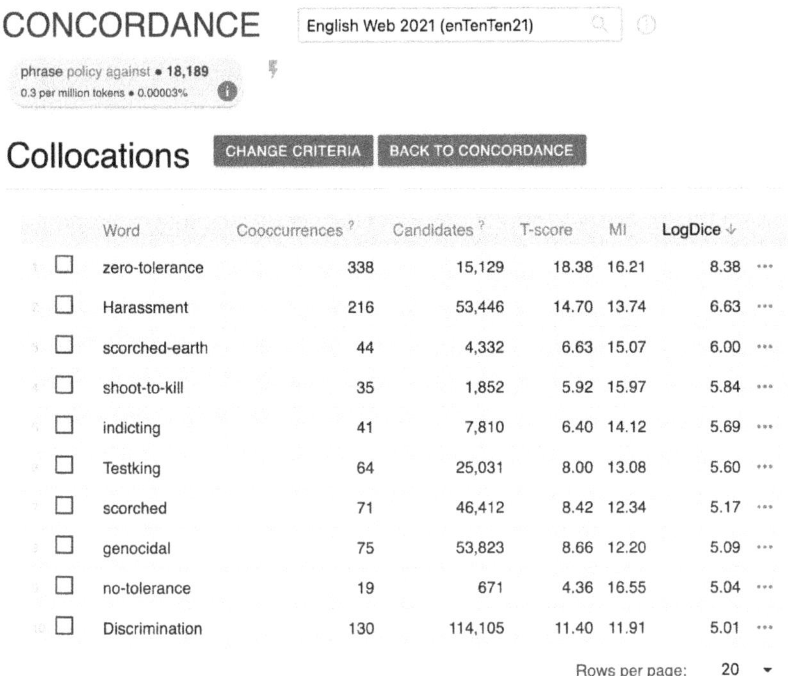

Figure 7 Collocations of *policy against* in the EnTenTen21
corpus on Sketch Engine

with: a simple text document or a web page (cf. Section 5). Start with finding occurrences of a word and simple frequencies. Use tools such as Google, CorpusMate, PlayPhrase, or YouGlish (see Section 5). They can be used in DDL-like ways and facilitate conversations around the role of frequency and pattern detection. In the same way, we suggest that it is best to try to understand which corpus software and which corpora work best for different query types, as well as for different student profiles, needs, and motivations in different teaching scenarios. Try various corpora and tools before bringing DDL to the classroom. Also, make sure you have selected some concordance lines to work with before the lesson. Save them to a pdf file or print them. You never know if the lab will be unavailable, the software down or the internet connection unstable, for whatever reason. Before a hands-on session, go through the basic queries you would like your students to use yourself, making sure they return the language you want to teach. If this is not the case, try to come up with a more refined query and improve to some extent the pedagogic quality of the resulting concordance lines you would like your students to work with.

• Plan your goals and procedures in advance

Be flexible in terms of your aims. Different students will approach hands-on DDL in different ways, and will come up with different types of queries and interpretations of the results. They may also bring their devices, mainly laptops, tablets or even smartphones (the advantage being that they are more likely to continue out of class). Make sure you have a sense of how your lesson may work on these devices. Learners who use concordances for translation, language learning, or as a reference resource show different preferences compared to those using concordances for teaching or linguistic research (Ballance, 2017). Learners who use concordancing as a reference tool use them as a quick and convenient resource for specific language-related tasks, usually a question about a specific language point. These learners typically seek examples that are directly relevant to their immediate needs, such as writing an essay, translating a text, or clarifying language usage. Language learners who follow the so-called analysis type model may need to discover language patterns inductively. They will be looking for information across multiple concordance lines to uncover broader patterns in the corpus. As previously seen in this section, this analytical approach involves a more systematic examination of concordance lines to gain a deeper understanding of language features and usage. This approach to DDL is characterised by a research-oriented and detailed exploration of language data. As a language teacher, be ready to think in advance what you expect from your students and be ready to anticipate the challenges or problems involved.

• Practice, repetition and multiple iterations

Hands-on DDL is challenging for most students. If hands-on DDL involves discovering patterns in the corpus, repeated practice is key. Students need to be shown how to do this, beginning with easy-to-identify patterns. Encourage the use of more than one single resource. Multiple interactions with different resources such as corpora and internet resources enhance the effectiveness of the searches. A few years ago, we were able to identify why B2-C1 learners of English found it hard to query the British National Corpus (BNC) by looking at the exact queries that the students used to answer questions about cleft sentences (Pérez-Paredes et al., 2012). Despite explicit training about the query interface for the BNC, a significant number of students either searched for the name of the grammatical structure ('clefts') in the BNC, or failed to use wildcards such as '*' or POS-tags as part of the query.[22] Although a combination of these may improve search results and their interpretation, our main finding was that the more successful learners behaved more like researchers by seeking additional

---

[22] Advanced searches can also be performed on www.google.es/advanced_search.

information to refine their queries. In this type of concordancing analysis, learners engaged in multiple BNC searches, consulted BNC guidelines, conducted searches on Google or similar search engines, and then returned to the BNC for further queries before completing the activity. Corpora should be used when they are useful – just as dictionaries and other resources also have their role to play.

2.7 Summary and Take-Home Message

This section has looked at the use of corpora, concordancers, and concordance lines in DDL. We have covered some of the most useful tools for DDL, as well as classroom tips and practical insights. We have emphasised the central role of language teachers in hands-on DDL. It is crucial for teachers to examine the concordance lines beforehand to avoid technical, linguistic, and pedagogical issues during the lesson. Teachers should test corpus queries to ensure they return the desired language and understand the purpose of the DDL activity from the learners' perspective.

3 Pedagogic Corpora and Younger Learners

3.1 Introduction

Most of what we know about the use of DDL comes from university settings. This is partly because lecturers are familiar with the use of corpora in their own research and to the availability of corpora such as the BNC or COCA (see Section 2), of interest to intermediate and advanced L2 English learners in undergraduate and graduate courses. However, there has been considerable progress in conceptualising DDL for younger learners over the past two decades (see e.g. Crosthwaite, 2019). In this context, discussions about language teachers' pedagogic mediation and pedagogic corpora (PCs) have been key.

One of the common themes in the discussions on how to transfer the potential of corpora for language learning to the classroom has been the collection and design of classroom-friendly corpora in secondary education. In this area, Sabine Braun's work has been influential in raising some of the central issues for using corpora with younger learners. In Braun (2005), she provided a rationale for using corpus data in secondary schools. Here is a breakdown of her assessment:

- Corpus data have the potential to present students with real-life language usage and naturally occurring patterns.
- A corpus is an excellent source for the exploration and selection of real patterns beyond the word level. Seeing examples in context can promote learners' acquisition of such patterns.

- Corpora can complement language materials (textbooks, dictionaries, and grammars, etc.) by providing alternative ways to show relevant examples of attested language use.
- Language teachers can understand how corpus data can complement more traditional materials in their own classroom context better than any other professional. They are best situated to make sense of how corpus-enhanced materials can be tailored to the needs and interests of their students.

For Braun, we need to revisit the concept of corpus itself rather than the type of analysis to be carried out, which is still that of language patterning. As we saw in Section 1, language patterns and pattern identification and analysis have attracted a great deal of attention in the research community as well as among professional materials developers (see the study by Curry et al., 2022, for an editorial perspective of how Cambridge University Press integrates corpus findings in their coursebooks).

3.2 The Role of the Teacher

The role of language teachers is critical in understanding the macro, meso, and micro contexts in which corpus data and DDL are used, offering concrete ways into the selection of DDL activities. Language teachers play a crucial role in this process as they are best placed to understand how corpus data can deliver the kind of learning and materials that their students need. Braun (2005) also suggests that teachers can provide guidance that helps their learners develop critical thinking skills and cultural awareness.

One of the main challenges for language teachers wishing to use corpora in their classroom is the integration of corpus consultation and activities in their syllabus. In a recent focus group with teachers of Spanish as a foreign language in the UK (Pérez-Paredes & Abad, 2025 in press), secondary-school language teachers showed their interest in the use of corpus data for teaching real language, while at the same time voicing concerns that their curriculum is to a great extent exam-driven, which deprives their students of opportunities to explore and learn in more creative ways. The following are quotes from feedback with this focus group, translated from Spanish into English:

- I am very interested in corpus linguistics and collocations and seeing which words go with which most frequently and teach students real use of the language. (Isabella)
- In my experience with A-level students [...] it is important to see how frequency and register work together [...], what we see in corpora we can analyse, like, we can see the contexts where words are used. (Betty)

- Everything is so focused on the exam that, somehow, students' autonomy is left aside. That's why I am so interested in the use of corpora [...] students discovering things. (Paula)

Tailoring activities to specific contexts and learner profiles is crucial for successful implementation of DDL. Also, corpora are excellent to test the language teachers' own intuitions about how language works across genres and situations of use. Research has shown that DDL activities frequently generate positive learning outcomes (Boulton & Cobb, 2017), in terms of language gains (e.g. vocabulary, grammar, error correction, etc.) or increased language awareness. In other words, we have enough evidence to show that DDL is effective. However, success depends largely on the mediation provided by the language teachers.

Pedagogic mediation (Braun, 2005) between the corpus used with the students and the learners' engagement with the activities and the materials designed by their language teachers is key. In instructed language learning contexts such as secondary schools, teachers are equipped with the necessary institutional knowledge to adapt corpus data to the official language curriculum in place. Because they know their students' proficiency and learning trajectories, teachers can streamline different activities or materials, for example curating concordance lines or devising tasks relevant to different language learners depending on their needs, proficiency levels, etc. Structuring and facilitating students' interactions with corpus materials can enhance the effectiveness and relevance of corpus-based activities in the classroom.

In a secondary school context, providing ad hoc activities and guidance helps students navigate and make sense of the language data available in the corpus. In the rest of this section, we discuss two scenarios where pedagogic corpora can foster secondary-school learners' language acquisition. The two scenarios show different approaches to the design, collection, and use of corpus data.

3.3 Scenario 1: Creating DDL Materials for Younger Language Learners

In this scenario, language teachers may either collect their own corpus data and design their own DDL materials, or adapt available corpora. The type of corpus data we will use here is from pedagogic corpora that are specifically designed for educational purposes, with a focus on supporting language learning and teaching.

3.3.1 Pedagogic Corpora

The progress that has been made in the last decade in the processing and storage capacity of natural language and multimedia files, as well as in the automatic recording and transcription of spoken texts, contributes to teaching practices where the design and compilation of a small corpus is more than feasible. Let us examine how language teachers can conceptualise and work with PCs.

Pedagogically relevant corpora and corpora as open educational resources (Vyatkina, 2020) are designed to support language learning and teaching, showing distinctive features that are not necessarily present in a general-purpose corpus such as the BNC or COCA (Braun, 2005, 2007; Pérez-Paredes, 2019; Vyatkina, 2020). These features include:

- PCs feature authentic, natural language use that is relevant to the language learners.
- PCs are not meant to be representative of a language variety or a community of speakers, as their primary users are not linguists or language researchers. PCs are representative of language that is relevant to learners during their learning trajectories.
- PCs may be annotated with pedagogically relevant information to support learners in interpreting language data, highlighting language features that are important for learners to grasp.
- PCs may include multimedia, multimodal elements such as audio, video, and supplementary information in the form of texts or hypermedia, encouraging language learners to explore language in a more interactive and engaging manner.
- PCs are specifically designed to be user-relevant and user-friendly. They should be designed to be easy to query and navigate for both learners and teachers.

A good starting point when considering the design of PCs is a focus on topics that are appropriate to language learners as texts in their own right: relevant themes can potentially make the language content more engaging and meaningful. There are several reasons why topics are important in corpora within the context of language learning and research. Firstly, topics can be aligned with the content covered in the language curriculum and textbook. This alignment can make corpus data more directly applicable to students' learning objectives (Braun, 2007; Meunier, 2019; Pérez-Paredes, 2019; Vyatkina, 2020). By selecting corpora that include texts related to specific topics or subject areas, educators can enhance the contextual relevance of language input for learners. In language education, small corpora do not aim for representative coverage, but rather are intended to cover specific areas or genres that are less represented in big corpora (e.g. the BNC), and which have immediate relevance for the intended learners.

Second, topics provide a context for language use within the corpus. This allows learners to explore how language patterns are employed in texts that are 'authenticated' (Mishan, 2004) against the learners' own learning experience. Relevant topics for secondary school learners such as hobbies, holidays, social media, future careers, or climate change can facilitate vocabulary acquisition by presenting words and phrases in contexts which may already be familiar. By incorporating topics that resonate with students' interests, experiences, and cultural backgrounds, teachers can create a more personalised and engaging learning experience. In addition, topics in such corpora enable researchers, educators, and learners themselves to analyse discourse patterns, genre conventions, and communicative strategies within specific thematic domains. This interest in themes and topics may be suitable and possibly more useful than the division into linguistic genres found in most representative corpora.

3.3.2 How to Design a Pedagogic Corpus

Pedagogic corpora serve as valuable resources for language educators to create relevant learning activities that may focus on a variety of language learning areas such as vocabulary, grammar and discourse patterns, as well as cultural aspects of language use (Hoffstaedter & Kohn, 2009). The design of pedagogic corpora follows a process (Pérez-Paredes, 2019) that starts with the definition of the purpose of the corpus and the selection of the data, and is followed by the annotation of the data, the organisation and delivery of the PCs and the integration of the learning activities. Table 6 introduces the stages involved in designing and collecting PCs.

PCs such as the SACODEYL corpora of teenage interviews and talk (Widmann et al., 2011) follow the stages in Table 6. SACODEYL was a pioneering corpus that sought to implement Braun's (2005, p. 61) conceptualisation that 'a coherent and relevant content, a restricted size, a multimedia format and a pedagogic annotation of the corpus' can facilitate the integration of pedagogically relevant enrichment materials in the secondary-school classroom. In other words, PCs can serve as first ports of call for the creation of further materials and resources including the integration of curriculum-driven contents. A pedagogically annotated corpus such as SACODEYL can give language teachers the opportunity to retrieve specific patterns and vocabulary. For example, a teacher may be interested in providing their students with input on the co-texts where *think* is used in spoken English. According to the corpus-driven *Longman Grammar of Spoken and Written English* (Biber et al., 1999), *think* is one of the most frequent and versatile verbs in conversation. In the SACODEYL data, we can explore the annotation added by EFL teachers and explore the use of the verb *think* when teenagers talk about future plans or jobs, and where some sort of modality is involved.[23]

---

[23] In Sketch Engine this involves a CQL search like the following [lemma='think'] within <div decls='#futurePlanTopic #Modality #Jobs'/>. More on both simple and complex searches can be found in Pérez-Paredes (2020).

Table 6 How to design a pedagogic corpus

Stage 1	Define the purpose of the pedagogic corpus	As a language teacher, outline the goals and objectives of the corpus. What do you want to achieve with it? Determine the target language proficiency level, linguistic features of interest, and the language skills involved (listening, speaking, reading, writing).
Stage 2	Select the data	Choose authentic language data that is relevant to the learners' needs and interests. This may include transcripts of spoken interactions, written texts, audio recordings, video clips, or a combination of these sources. Ensure that the collected data represent a variety of genres or sociolinguistic variables (e.g. male and female speakers, age range, and accents) of potential interest to your learners.
Stage 3	Examine and, where appropriate, annotate the data	Add annotations to the corpus to highlight key linguistic features such as target word classes or contractions, cultural references such as proper names or festivities, and discourse structures such as backchannelling or cohesive discourse markers. Annotations may include glosses, translations, explanations of idiomatic expressions, grammatical analyses, and instructions for language practice and further learning.
Stage 4	Organise the corpus	Structure the corpus in a way that allows easy access to different types of language data and annotations. You may consider categorising the data based on themes, topics, language functions, or proficiency levels to facilitate targeted language learning activities. Ideally, stages 3 and 4 should be conducted in unison.

Table 6 (cont.)

| Stage 5 | Think 'learning' | Create language learning tasks and exercises that are based on the content of the pedagogic corpus. Design activities that focus on vocabulary expansion, grammar practice, listening comprehension, speaking tasks, writing assignments, and cultural exploration. Ensure that the activities align with the learning objectives of the corpus and, when relevant, with the syllabus. |
| Stage 6 | Corpus delivery and technology | Use digital tools and platforms to make sure that the corpus can be accessed by learners. If feasible, create multimedia and collaborative features to engage learners in meaningful language practice and communication. |

Figure 8 shows some of the most frequent adverbs in the English SACODEYL corpus.[24] The corpus is not large at all, comprising just 58,000 words. However, the language collected in the twenty-five interviews reflects topics that most secondary EFL syllabuses follow, which creates the conditions for both authentic and authenticated uses of interest to language learners.

Really is the third most common adverb in the corpus. Figure 9 shows some of the 400-plus concordance lines where it is used by the teenagers interviewed. This gives both teachers and students the opportunity to explore different contexts and pragmatic uses of *really*, including the expression of degree, sceptical responses, factual meanings, hedging and concessive meaning.

Some of these uses of *really* are rarely represented in language textbooks, and even when they are, learners are usually deprived of the extended context where they occur, offering an impoverished input. The search options are endless. Language teachers can either download SACODEYL in English, French,

---

[24] Part-of-Speech (POS) tagging identifies every word in a corpus as belonging to a specific part of speech, such as nouns or verbs. The tag for adverbs also includes some conjunctions such as *that*, which explains why it is found in Figure 8. For an introduction to POS tags and tagging see Pérez-Paredes (2020).

WORDLIST

SACODEYL EN Clean

adverb (247 items | 5,686 total frequency)

	Adverb	Frequency ?↓			Adverb	Frequency ?↓	
1	not	660	•••	11	there	123	•••
2	so	522	•••	12	much	86	•••
3	really	453	•••	13	now	81	•••
4	yeah	426	•••	14	also	78	•••
5	just	340	•••	15	actually	77	•••
6	well	251	•••	16	more	73	•••
7	then	226	•••	17	as	69	•••
8	quite	179	•••	18	always	58	•••
9	very	174	•••	19	sometimes	57	•••
10	about	129	•••	20	maybe	52	•••

Figure 8 Most frequent adverbs in the English SACODEYL corpus

German, Lithuanian, Romanian, and Spanish or check them out on Sketch Engine.[25] The internet, with its huge store of freely available texts, has made it vastly easier to create PCs; at the same time, it can still be complex and time-consuming to collect, process and provide a corpus for use in the classroom, which may discourage some teachers. In two relatively recent European surveys, language teachers in the UK and Spain said that they rarely made use of corpus management tools such as Sketch Engine or AntConc, compared to online dictionaries (Pérez-Paredes et al., 2018). In a replication study just five years later (Kic-Drgas et al., 2023), language teachers in Poland and Turkey said that they used corpus management tools a few times per academic year, which may suggest that corpora are becoming more popular among language teachers across the board.

The good news for language teachers is that there are now plenty of resources that can be useful to learn some of the skills needed to put together a corpus. Below, we provide just a few pointers that could be a good first step for teachers wishing to explore the collection and use of their own pedagogic corpora.

---

[25] Respectively www.perezparedes.es/sacodeyl-xml-corpora and www.sketchengine.eu.

Figure 9 Concordance lines of *really* in the English SACODEYL corpus

3.3.3 Selecting the Data

Textual data may be relatively easy to obtain. Video portals such as YouTube offer transcriptions of some of the videos which can be usefully harvested for some purposes. Many institutions offer free-to-use materials that can be relevant across teaching sites and scenarios. While most countries allow use of extracts for educational purposes, it is generally a good idea to explore the copyright restrictions of these materials (as indeed any others), and the way to obtain permission, if necessary, in your own school context. Also, it is important that teachers consider whether the content and the type of language in the videos selected is appropriate and whether the videos contain the use of potentially offensive or taboo language, etc.

A language teacher wishing to put together a Spanish language pedagogic corpus of, for example, values in sports, can find hundreds of talks and interviews on the topic, covering different types of interactive situations as well as genres. Figure 10 shows a transcript from a TED Talk video[26] where Toni Nadal, Rafael Nadal's uncle and first coach, talks about values such as effort, sacrifice, perseverance and respect. This is a slow-paced talk which lasts 18 minutes and is made up of some 2,800 words.

Many videos on YouTube offer supervised, quality transcriptions like the one in Figure 10. Creating a small corpus is relatively straightforward if the video has subtitles. These are the steps to follow:

1. Find and access YouTube Transcriptions
   a. Go to the YouTube video(s) you want to use.
   b. Click on the menu below the video or in the video player controls and click 'Open transcript.'

2:20   Yo creo que cuando uno

2:22   **no se sabe suficientemente bueno y conoce la realidad,**

2:26   es el primer paso, es el punto de partida, para alcanzar los propósitos.

2:32   Así lo he entendido yo siempre.

2:35   He rehuido siempre de una sobrevaloración

Figure 10 Transcript from Toni Nadal's talk on effort in sports

---

[26] https://youtu.be/FXL2G1p-EDw?si=GDZUgpjmMUIFhfXY.

2. Extract the transcription

   a. Copy the text from the transcript window. If the transcript includes timestamps, you may want to remove them later.

3. Organise and save the transcriptions

   a. Open a text editor such as Notepad on a Windows machine or TextEdit on a Mac and paste the copied transcript; save as a txt file.

   b. If needed, remove any timestamps or unnecessary information to keep only the spoken text.

4. Save and store your corpus

   a. Create a dedicated folder on your computer to store all the transcription files; name the files consistently for easy identification.

   b. If you have multiple files, you may want to combine them into a single one or keep them as separate files, depending on your analysis needs.

The corpus can be queried using AntConc or similar software. Teachers can then select relevant instances of language use and develop *ad hoc* materials for their students. To do this, it is likely that the texts will have to be prepared, as explained above. Cleaning the text data is also relatively easy, though may be time consuming: clean as much as you need, but no more. This process entails removing irrelevant or misleading elements from the files such as metadata or unnecessary characters. ChatGPT or text tools such as ConvertCase[27] can help with removing line breaks or time-stamps, etc. If your programming skills are up to it, you may also benefit from some relatively easy-to-use Python scripts that can manipulate your text in all sorts of ways in next to no time. Additionally, corpus data can be annotated[28] with relevant information that can be searched by language learners.

3.3.4 Corpus Delivery and Technology

The use of digital tools and platforms enhances the usability and interactivity of PCs. Language teachers may be interested in incorporating multimedia such as links to YouTube videos, interactive exercises, online forums, and collaborative features that engage their students in meaningful language practice. This can be done in multiple ways, the most obvious include:

---

[27] https://convertcase.net.

[28] If a corpus has been annotated, searches can benefit from data categorisation. For example, in Sketch Engine we can add metadata that shows the nationality of the speakers, or the variety spoken, the range of topics, the year when a text was recorded or written, the gender of the speaker, the name of the publication, target structures of interest to language learners, etc.

- Using an institution's virtual learning platform such as Moodle or similar.
- Developing material and publishing it online. Software such as WordPress is free to download and use, providing templates to start with. Text, pictures, and embedded YouTube videos can be easily combined, together with exercises that can be created using flashcards or multiple choice questions plugins.

Language teachers can find here an opportunity to explore their creativity and maybe join other teachers to share resources and discuss the use of this type of materials. The EUROCALL CorpusCALL Special Interest Group is a great starting point.[29]

3.4 Scenario 2: Younger Learners Using Language Data in the Classroom

In this scenario, we examine how primary-school learners and secondary-school learners have used DDL across contexts, showcasing a selection of activities chosen by the teachers in their application of DDL.

3.4.1 Learning English with Very Young Learners of English in Japan

It is rare to find accounts of DDL being used with very young learners during the last years of primary education or the early years of secondary school. One exception is Spivey (2023), who used DDL with 11- and 12-year-olds in a Japanese elementary school. The Japanese children learnt verb and noun combinations such as *like pizza* or *study science* extracted from their regular coursebooks. The learners used printed concordance lines, online corpora and the DDL-Study website[30] which offers ready-to-use activities. Figure 11 shows the web interface used in Spivey (2023) to generate activities and a sample of the grammar areas available to language teachers.

Spivey adopted a light DDL approach where his main aim was for young learners to develop an interest in the use of concordance lines. He used the activity in Figure 12 to showcase different examples of sentences containing *went*, which could be heard and compared to a translation found adjacent to the English sentence. Students were then invited to colour the verbs and the nouns (e.g. *went*, *sea*, *week* on line 34).

3.4.2 A Secondary School in Germany

One of the first documented uses of DDL with young L2 learners is from Braun (2007). In her study, twenty-five secondary-school students in Germany engaged in activities from ELISA (the English Language Interview corpus as

---

Figure 11 Web interface of DDL activities for Japanese learners of English reported in Spivey (2023)

Figure 12 A DDL activity from the experiment included in Spivey (2023) showing simplified concordance lines and translations

a Second-language Application), a corpus of narrative interviews with L1 English speakers of different varieties of English including the United States, Australia, England, and Scotland. The interviews were recorded and the audio track transcribed. The speakers talk about their professional careers and discuss different fields of education and training, covering a similar range of topics, including a description of their professions, educational background, daily routines, and future plans. These are all issues of general interest in professional contexts such as their motivations and the kind of work they do:

> The main point about ELISA is that it covers a variety of communicatively relevant topics from the broad area of professional, social and cultural life. According to the CEF it can be said to reflect relevant uses of language in the occupational and personal domains. (Braun, 2006, p. 30)

The transcribed text and the video files were available online and the language learners had access to the DDL activities through Moodle. The activities developed included the analysis of concordance lines from the interviews, the exploration of wordlists, and ad hoc computer-based exercises. The use of the ELISA corpus and the DDL activities were conceptualised as part of the students' curriculum. For example, one group of activities covered contents on Australia, life in Australia and working in Australia, with the steps outlined in Table 7 (Braun, 2007).

The interviews were first watched in class, leading to a group discussion. After watching the second interview, the learners were randomly assigned to one of two groups: one group, as control, completed traditional activities such as explanations and gap-fill versions of the relevant section of the interview transcript; the other group, the experimental group, worked on corpus-based activities. As in the SACODEYL corpus, interviews were divided into small topic-driven sections. Each section of the second interview was assigned two different sets of activities (traditional vs. corpus-based). The materials in the DDL group (Braun, 2007, p. 312) included:

- Frequency lists of the words used in each interview.
- Ready-made concordances from the two interviews watched by the students, 'but complemented [. . .] by selected "clear-cut" examples from other interviews' (p. 312).

Table 7 Introducing DDL in a secondary-school class (Braun, 2007)

1. Warming up. Introduction to Australia. Use of visuals from the textbook, a presentation and a class discussion.
2. Use of one of the ELISA interviews with an Australian speaker of English on migration.
3. Work with short texts and exercises from the textbook about Australia's past and present, including migration and cultural heritage.
4. Use of the second ELISA interview with an Australian speaker of English on cultural heritage in Australia.
5. Group presentations on individual aspects of Australia.

- Full concordances of each interview, including a complete wordlist of the interview and the option to see a KWIC concordance of it (see Section 2). Examples of such concordances included *job*, *get to*, and *move + PREPOSITION*. These concordances and target vocabulary were chosen by the language teacher, and the selection was devised as a complement to the official textbook and curriculum.

Questionnaires showed that the students in the DDL group found that corpus-based activities made them more successful language learners and rated DDL activities as more useful than traditional ones. In particular, the DDL group stated that they had learnt 'very much' or 'much' about English grammar, whereas the control group did not feel that their traditional activities afforded the same in-depth learning experience. However, the students in the DDL group faced some problems with the interpretation of wordlists and concordances. For Braun (2007), such interpretation demands a level of analytical skills and attention to detail that the short period of time devoted to DDL did not provide.

3.4.3 Improving Phraseological Competence

Phraseological competence is the language learners' ability to understand and use multi-word lexical units such as collocations, lexical bundles (also known as n-grams, chunks or clusters) or idioms. Szudarski (2019) designed DDL activities to enhance the phraseological knowledge of twenty-two L1 Polish secondary-school learners of English. He put together printed concordance lines of fifteen phrasal units from the BNC (see Section 2) and distributed them to the students. The phrasal units included, among others, *at all, take over, other than, by far, is likely to, as of, by no means* and *take for granted*. Szudarski was interested in testing whether DDL could actually work for secondary-school learners, so a control group used a dictionary instead of the printed concordance lines. Both groups showed language gains, as expected. However, and this was the main point behind the experiment, DDL showed itself as a valuable complementary approach to other materials such as textbooks and dictionaries. Szudarski notes that the use of printed concordance lines with lower-proficiency students is viable in secondary education, which opens further avenues of work with hands-on DDL and corpus interfaces.

3.5 Summary and Take-Home Message

This section has shown how secondary-school language teachers can use corpora in their classrooms, sharing some ideas for putting together pedagogic corpora and stressing the need to pick the right data and understand learners' needs. DDL allows teachers to create or adapt teaching materials based on authentic language use, making lessons more relevant and engaging for students. By using real examples, teachers can illustrate language patterns and usage more effectively. The section also looks at how younger learners can work with language data in the classroom, giving examples from different educational settings. Language teachers can customise DDL activities to meet the specific needs and proficiency levels of their students. This adaptability ensures that all learners can engage with the materials in a way that is appropriate for their individual learning trajectories

4 Data-Driven Learning at University: The Case of Academic Writing

4.1 Introduction

It is a well-known truism that English for Academic Purposes or EAP is nobody's first language. Nevertheless, the skills for writing academic English are not always taught explicitly, despite a genuine need during university courses and beyond, where professionals need to understand and produce academic or disciplinary texts – so much so that it has even been given its own acronym: ERPP, standing for English for Research Publication Purposes. Traditionally, the thinking has been that reading alone will provide sufficient encounters for vocabulary and expressions, grammar, style and structure to sink in by osmosis, and then be available for productive purposes. There is no doubt an element of truth in this, but that does not mean that it works equally well for all people, or that we cannot speed up the process by overt teaching or sensitisation. DDL is well placed for this as it promotes noticing language in context by making various features salient, and (given an appropriate corpus and skillset) allows for individualisation of queries depending on the specific needs, discipline, and so on.

Many university courses require students to read and write English, especially at graduate level, reflecting the perceived status of English as a *lingua franca* for specific and academic purposes (ESP, EAP). Although much valuable research is (and should be) published in a range of languages, it has been estimated that 90 per cent or more of academic publications are in English (Curry & Lillis, 2024). For speakers of other languages, English can be considered an obstacle, even a kind of gate-keeping to exclude outsiders. The barrier is clearly not insurmountable, since the majority of academic publication in English is not by 'native' English speakers (Hyland, 2016); but it does come at a price in terms of extra time and individual effort (Amano et al., 2023). Indeed, for an academic corpus to be representative, it is essential that it include texts by speakers of other languages who vastly outnumber speakers of English as a first language.

So why is 'language' important in academia – surely it is the scientific content of a paper that matters? Formal problems including language can distract the reader, and are more likely to lead to reviewers recommending a paper be rejected (Tschichold et al., 2024). This is especially true of writing, in all types of contexts: in conference presentations, participants may be distracted by errors on the slides more than in the spoken commentary, whatever the accent or L1 of the presenter. The appearance of GenAI tools to edit texts may already be helping open publication up further, though that brings problems of its own, both ethical and pedagogical, as we shall see in Section 5. In particular, users of GenAI tools such as ChatGPT must accept responsibility for the text in their own name, so really need to check each suggestion; this is clearly also essential for any learning to take place.

So while English may seem an unnecessary burden to students (and to some teachers), EAP courses should aim to prepare students to function in real-world contexts. This is no mean feat, especially with multidisciplinary groups. For a variety of reasons, there has been a wealth of research on academic writing, especially research articles, a lot of it corpus-based. It should be noted that criteria for inclusion in such corpora depend on many things but rarely 'native-speaker' status: the important point is that the article was successfully published. Among the best-known is work by Swales and colleagues; of particular interest here is the book *Academic Writing for Graduate Students* (Swales & Feak, 2010). Based on a collection of journals in different disciplines, this describes many aspects of research articles (RAs), from overall structure to specific language features. Among the former, they present the standard IMRAD model (Introduction, Methods, Results and Discussion), and the CARS model for introductions (Create A Research Space). There are also tendencies at the micro-level, with relatively higher use of present tenses in the Introduction and Conclusion sections, for example, and past tenses in the Methods and Results. However, the authors take pains to point out that these are usual and transdisciplinary features, and should not be seen as normative models that every paper has to be forced into.

4.2 The Potential of Corpora for Teaching Academic Writing

Other corpus-based work includes the attempt to devise lists of potentially useful academic language, beginning with Coxhead's (2000) Academic Word List (AWL). Though this has since been criticised, the aim of providing a focused list across a broad range of disciplines is laudable, and can help make learning more manageable. Other attempts have taken this further, such as Gardner and Davies' (2014) New Academic Vocabulary List, which claims twice the coverage of the AWL and can be downloaded or explored online.[31] In other tools, the user can upload a text and have all the academic words highlighted.[32] Simpson-Vlach and Ellis (2010) devised an Academic Formulas List, i.e. recurrent patterns and n-grams found in a range of genres. Also on the premise that academic vocabulary does not exist in a vacuum, Ackermann and Chen (2013) proposed their Academic Collocation List: ADJECTIVE + NOUN combinations account for over 70 per cent of the entries, reflecting the dominance of noun phrases in academic writing. It is also possible for students to compile their own corpora and produce wordlists themselves (e.g. Smith, 2020). All these resources have a different function to specialised dictionaries: they can serve as a reference but may more usefully be seen as learning tools – knowing what should be taught and learned. Such interdisciplinary reference lists have considerable potential in EAP teaching, though once established, there is no need for the activities based on them to differ from traditional vocabulary teaching. That said, Cobb (forthcoming) argues strongly that 'word lists have been left out of the DDL conversation [. . . but potentially] are as much a part of DDL as concordances'.

Various types of academic corpora exist. In Section 2, we looked at some corpora widely used in general purpose English language teaching. Spoken language is beyond the scope of this section, but for those wishing to follow up, it is worth mentioning MICASE[33] and BASE,[34] the Michigan and British Academic Spoken English corpora. Their written counterparts, MICUSP[35] and BAWE[36] (the Michigan Corpus of Upper-Level Student Papers and the British Academic Written English corpus) comprise written assignments at university level; as they are written by students rather than by professionals, they may be more amenable for some purposes. And even though they were compiled some years ago, it is not the content so much as the language used that is important, and that is less likely to date quickly. MICUSP can be consulted online, the interface providing filters for level (first-year undergraduates, etc.), native vs non-native writers, paper types (argumentative, research report, etc.), and especially discipline (a total of 16). BAWE was constructed on the same

---

[31] www.academicwords.info.   [32] www.eapfoundation.com/vocab/academic/nawlhighlighter.

[33] https://quod.lib.umich.edu/cgi/c/corpus/corpus?c=micase;page=simple.

[34] www.coventry.ac.uk/research/research-directories/current-projects/2015/british-academic-spoken-english-corpus-base/search-the-base-corpus.

[35] https://elicorpora.info/main.

[36] www.coventry.ac.uk/research/research-directories/current-projects/2015/british-academic-written-english-corpus-bawe/search-the-bawe-corpus.

lines and can be accessed via LexTutor[37] (which offers other specialised corpora) or downloaded for use offline.

Most academic corpora however are compiled from RAs, which are abundantly available in electronic format and represent an important genre for novice writers. Unfortunately, as most RAs are copyright protected, this means that the collections themselves are rarely downloadable and can only be consulted online via dedicated interfaces; we consider some of these in the following section. The upside however is that it has encouraged a DIY mentality of producing one's own academic corpus which, though small, will be far more specific than any compiled by others; we return to this in the final section of this section.

EAP writing is a key topic in DDL: in a collection of abstracts from 718 empirical DDL studies, 53 mention 'academic writing' – 29 in the last 5 years alone (2019–23). This aligns with Boulton and Vyatkina (2024), who found an increase in EAP in their collection of empirical DDL research articles from prestige journals, from 25 to 45 per cent of the annual total in recent years (2018–22). DDL papers for academic purposes divide into two broad areas: relatively controlled teacher-fronted activities focusing on specific language items using a published corpus, and working more openly with learners' individual writing needs and their own DIY corpora. We address each in turn in the following sections.

4.3 Scenario 1: DDL for General Academic Purposes

General resources provide general information: they have their uses in all areas of language teaching, but a specific need can benefit from a specific resource – just as general language dictionaries can be complemented by ones in law, medicine, engineering, and so on. Some even make a distinction between English for General and Specific Academic Purposes (EGAP and ESAP, respectively). For some purposes, a DDL approach to academic language can draw on quite general corpora and tools which may lend themselves to whole-class activities with a specific language focus and known outcomes: the teacher remains in control. They will decide in advance to focus on a given language point such as vocabulary and lexicogrammar (collocations, chunks), linking adverbials, reporting verbs, and so on, with many research studies of this type.

4.3.1 General Corpora for EGAP

One of the most widely used general corpora, the Corpus of Contemporary American English (COCA) (Davies, 2009; see Section 2), can be searched

---

HELP			ALL FORMS (SAMPLE): 100 200 500	FREQ	TOTAL 5,561 | UNIQUE 1,053 +
1			A SIGNIFICANT EFFECT	569	
2			A POSITIVE EFFECT	362	
3			A MAIN EFFECT	278	
4			A NEGATIVE EFFECT	239	
5			A LARGE EFFECT	129	
6			A PROFOUND EFFECT	125	
7			A SMALL EFFECT	114	
8			A DIRECT EFFECT	90	
9			AN ADVERSE EFFECT	89	
10			A SIMILAR EFFECT	79	

Figure 13 Results for *a/an * effect* in COCA

by section, one of which is ACADEMIC. The 2020 update included texts from over 200 different peer-reviewed journals in 'the full range of academic disciplines',[38] and can be queried as a whole or by sub-section, from humanities to science and technology. As with any tool, a little caution is needed: where learners used to say 'but I found it in the dictionary', now it is 'but I found it in the corpus'. The user should always take a step back and consider whether the results make sense as they are, or need pursuing further for the specific context. The most basic query involves simply typing a word into the box, but can include the hugely useful 'wildcard' asterisk, which represents any complete word if there is a space either side of it. The query *a/an * effect* will bring up examples of words between the article and the noun, which can be useful when trying to think of synonyms, or checking if two words actually collocate. Figure 13 gives the first 10 possibilities, with a typical distribution pattern shown on the right; this 'Zipfian curve' indicates that the most common occurrences are indeed very common, but rapidly reduce in frequency so that items further down the list may be possible, but are not usual. It is crucial for the learner to appreciate this: even though *a favourable effect* is possible (frequency = 17), it is less likely *than a positive effect* (f = 362).

In general, it is worth checking some examples in context by clicking on the result shown as grey bars. The output in Figure 14 clearly shows that *a significant effect* is associated with statistical results, so in academic writing should perhaps not be used unless backed up by statistics. However, these are all from the same journal: choosing SAMPLE: *100* ensures a random selection.

The asterisk has a second function when attached to a word or string of letters: thus the search term *help* simply provides occurrences of this word, while **help** might produce *helped, helper* or *unhelpful,* among others. Most variable words are lemmatised in COCA so it is possible to search for all terms

---

[38] www.english-corpora.org/coca/help/coca2020_overview.pdf.

research has found that the animacy of the sentential subjects or objects had a significant effect on the comprehension of relativ

1age # The results of logistic mixed-effects regression modeling indicated that there was a significant effect of age, beta =1.40, SE

1 =1.40, SE = 0.19, z =7.44, p <.05, a significant effect of RC type, beta =-0.30, SE =0.11, z =-2.70, p

1mmarized in Table 5. In the relative clause segment, there was a significant effect of age, beta =-0.45, SE =0.09, t =-4.92, p <.05

2eta =-0.45, SE =0.09, t =-4.92, p <.05, a significant effect of RC type, beta =0.04, SE =0.02, t =1.65, p

er de are summarized in Table 6. In these segments, we found a significant effect of age, beta = -0.49, SE =0.08, t =-5.84, p

analysis for main clause subjects. In this segment, there was a significant effect of age, beta =-0.55, SE =0.09, t =-5.99, p <.05

2eta =-0.55, SE =0.09, t =-5.99, p <.05, a significant effect of RC type, beta =0.01, SE =0.02, t =0.45, p

Table 8 shows, in the main verb segment, there was a significant effect of age, beta =-0.54, SE =0.09, t =-5.95, p <.05

tically significant (p >.05). In the younger group, there was a significant effect of sentence type in the inanimate condition (p <.05),

Figure 14 Contexts for *a significant effect* in COCA (academic)

of the verb *help* (*help, helps, helped, helping*) by inputting *HELP_V*, where the capitals mean all forms of the word, and *_V* means as a verb (thus excluding *help* as a noun). The main parts of speech (see Section 3) can be found in the POS box to the right: if they are separated by a space, then they represent a separate word, so that *help V* gives examples of *help* followed by a verb (*help explain, help reduce*, etc.). COCA provides many more features which can only be seen by clicking the + sign at the top of the page. One of the most useful is collocates, with the same features as above for choosing part of speech. For example, a learner unsure when to use the word *amount* can type in this word and choose only noun collocates within a window of four words to the right. The top ten in the ACADEMIC subcorpus are *time, information, money, variance, water, data, energy, work, research,* and *material*. The learner who thinks about these may notice that they are all uncountable, which is indeed typical of the use of *amount*.

Some searches need to be conducted in stages: think of a learner seeking to clarify in their own mind the difference between near synonyms like *big* and *large*, where dictionaries are unhelpfully circular. Using the Compare feature in the ACADEMIC subcorpus shows that most nouns to the right of *large* are measurable (*large extent, large proportion, large quantities*, etc.), while those to the right of *big* tend to be conceptually big or important, or relatively fixed phrases (*big bang, big deal, big brother*, etc.). But this is not the whole story, as the learner knows that the words often are indeed synonymous: part of their difference lies in the distribution or register. This can be checked using the Chart feature in COCA: *large* occurs 366 times per million words (pmw) in the ACADEMIC subcorpus, over four times as frequent as *big* (87 pmw); conversely, *big* is five times as frequent as *large* in the SPOKEN subcorpus (638 vs 123 pmw).

All such queries in COCA can be conducted online or copied for printed materials, or an intermediary solution adopted. Every search produces its own hyperlink which can be communicated to students so that they simply click on it and see the parameters already set; their job is then only to interpret the results.[39] This is particularly useful in the case of marking student writing: instead of providing a correction *per se*, learners can be shown the data necessary to arrive at the conclusion themselves, which requires some thinking on their part (thus more chance that it will be remembered), and seeing the query may help them improve their own search techniques. Gaskell and Cobb proposed similar procedures in 2004, and BAWE integrated a *quicklinks*[40] feature in the interface.

4.3.2 Simpler Tools for EGAP

If this still seems quite complex, there are even simpler tools for academic writing, including Hyper Collocation,[41] which is based on over 800,000 papers from the arXiv repository, especially for 'hard' sciences. The interface has only one entry box and one option: sort for the first word to the left (previous) or the right (next). So a search for *criticised* shows that the most frequent words to the right are *by* and *for*; the most frequent to the left are *been* and *was*. These may not be the most relevant, but we quickly come to adverbs such as *strongly, severely, heavily* or *widely criticized* – but not, for example, *highly criticized* on this list, even though *highly critical* certainly exists. A specific search shows that there are actually six occurrences of *highly criticized*, highlighting the importance of frequency: six occurrences in 800 k papers is fairly rare, and novice writers might be advised to avoid it. As before, unless the results give an obvious answer (akin to: 'of course, I knew that, why didn't I think of it?'), it is advisable to check contexts. This is possible in Hyper Collocation just by clicking the word, with samples shown in Figure 15 (the text image on the right takes the user to the original paper).

A number of tools have been developed for corpus-assisted writing, which feature corpora behind the scenes rather than up front, one such being ColloCaid.[42] The basic idea is to start typing an academic text, and the system underlines items that are in its database. These serve as prompts that can be opened to reveal typical patterns for the underlined words. An example is given in Figure 16, from typing in *The use of corpora in language learning* . . . . The word *use* is underlined so can be clicked on to reveal a series of boxes for *use* as a noun or verb, then typical collocates of the chosen form, and finally examples

---

[39] The search for *a/an* * *effect* can be found here: www.english-corpora.org/coca/?c=coca&q=
120867443.
[40] https://bawequicklinks.coventry.domains.   [41] https://hypcol.marutank.net.
[42] https://collocaid.uk.

Figure 15 Hyper Collocation for left collocates of *criticized*, developed for two adverbs

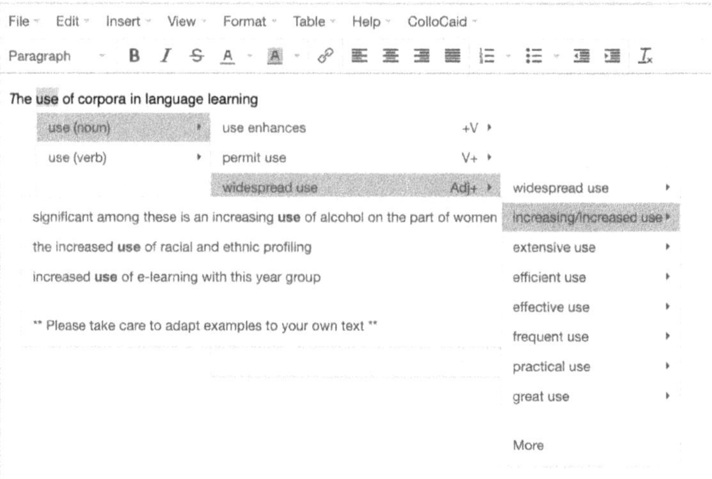

Figure 16 Prompt sequence for use in ColloCaid

from context, akin to a short concordance. Selecting one will add it directly to the text, though given the specific context, it is probably better to treat them as suggestions and keep typing the text manually – in other words, to continue with the noticing and decision-making that is part and parcel of DDL. The tool is described in further detail in Frankenberg-Garcia et al. (2019, 2022). A workshop introducing ColloCaid and other tools to fourteen teachers found that all but one continued using it a year later, more than any other tool except for dictionaries. This approach is transparent and leaves more choice in the hands of the user than GenAI (see Section 5).

4.4 Scenario 2: DDL for Specific Academic Purposes

The previous segment explored some uses of large, publicly available general corpora of academic language, which begs a number of questions. First, how specific does a corpus need to be for academic purposes? Chen et al. (2023) compared COCA (1 billion words) and a multidisciplinary corpus of 500 million words compiled using AntCorGen[43] and searchable with their own n-gram tool. The final results showed no significant difference between the two. However, the self-compiled corpus was also multidisciplinary, and did not draw on the AntCorGen option to create a corpus in one or more main

---

[43] All software created by Laurence Anthony referred to in this section can be downloaded free from www.laurenceanthony.net/software.html.

disciplines based on papers published the journal *PLOS ONE*. But it is possible to go further and for each learner/user to create their own corpus of papers they actually need to read and probably already have in electronic format (cf. Section 3). This relieves teachers of the burden of making these decisions on their behalf, and opens up a whole new realm of possibility, including for languages other than English where few resources are available. Students' familiarity with the contents of the corpus can be helpful, the results perceived to be more relevant, and being involved in the compilation stage can encourage a sense of involvement and ownership of the corpus, as well as increasing specificity.

While asking students to compile their own corpus may sound ambitious, numerous studies have shown that it is actually quite a realistic prospect – daunting at the start, but often highly rewarding, as we have found with our own students. Boulton (2024) describes teaching corpus linguistics to master's students of English who tend to be more at ease with the qualitative research in their fields of literature or cultural studies. The course required them to create their own corpus to address questions which they themselves defined, and they appreciated the freedom this allows. A survey of reactions at the start and end of the course almost invariably shift from such words as *daunting, scared,* and *overwhelmed* to *rewarding, enriching,* and even *addicted* (Boulton, 2024). Pérez-Paredes, Aguado-Jiménez, & Ordoñana-Guillamón (2025) worked with undergraduate students who, as learners of English themselves, were asked to approach the analysis of mass-media corpora to understand how public figures and social issues were represented in public discourse. They worked on projects dealing with small corpora of around 250,000 words and mastered the basics of corpus compilation and analysis, which can provide future language teachers with experience with corpus data interpretation and corpus data management.

Among the best-known research in this field is from Maggie Charles, who has published a series of papers based around her elective academic writing workshops for post-graduate students in the UK. Her first attempts were relatively controlled, focusing on rhetorical functions, but she soon allowed students greater liberty in compiling their own corpus of RAs and pursuing their own questions using AntConc, which was introduced during her six-week course of two-hour weekly sessions. Reporting on more than 500 participants from 50 iterations over nine years, she had the foresight to collect questionnaires not only at the start and end of the course, but also a year later. After a year, the students split evenly into thirds: regular autonomous corpus users (once a week or more), occasional users, and non-users (Charles & Hadley, 2022). Reasons for non-use were largely lack of need: while the participants originally chose the course because they had to write their master's or doctoral theses, the approach was abandoned when such needs evaporated (Charles, 2022).

Charles chose AntConc (see Section 2) as a relatively straightforward toolkit appropriate for smallish corpora such as students are likely to compile of RAs. Though version 4 accepts pdfs, in our experience it is still generally better to convert to txt format (UTF-8) using AntFileConverter, followed by minimal cleaning (metadata, references, etc.). The corpus can be stored using the corpus manager and then opened at the click of a button; a series of 10 short video tutorials on YouTube provides a clear overview of how the different tools work. The tutorials are essential to avoid numerous minor difficulties, but really are all the guidance that most users will need: the main learning process is heuristic – simply playing with the tool and a collection of texts. Charles (2018) also itemises the uses of each AntConc tool (version 3) from the perspective of academic writing.

4.4.1 Building and Exploring an ESAP Corpus

Continuing with AntConc v4, the examples in this section draw on a collection of RAs published in JCR-ranked journals[44] which feature the most visible empirical studies of DDL (expanding on synthesis papers by Boulton & Vyatkina, 2021, 2024). At 1.2 million words, the corpus of 191 studies is far larger (and cleaner) than most students would compile: Charles' students typically had between 10 and 19 RAs for under 200,000 words, and some DDL studies have proved revealing with just a few thousand words, depending on the contents and text types. Though tempting to search for specific items immediately, much can be learned as a first step from the AntConc Word list tool. Unsurprisingly, the most frequent items are grammar-function words (*the, of, and, to, in*), but the top twenty already include some content words (*corpus, students, language*), giving an idea of what the corpus is 'about'. To focus on the latter, a stoplist such as the most frequent items from the BNC can be applied; and if relevant, a lemmatiser can group inflected items, and the corpus can be tagged for part of speech, as discussed above.[45]

Common groups of words can be identified using the AntConc n-gram tool (it helps to set for minimum frequency or minimum range, that is the number of files a word occurs in, to speed things up and avoid idiosyncratic writing styles). The most frequent 4-gram (Figure 17) is *on the other hand* (227 occurrences in 97 files – over half the papers); learners might note that *on (the) one hand* does not occur, even though they have often been taught the two together as an

---

[44] Journal Citation Reports are produced annually by Clarivate Analytics, ranking journals by their impact factor (IF) in different disciplines. The IF is calculated as the number of citations in year X to full articles published in that journal in the preceding two years.

[45] Tools for all these operations can be found on Laurence Anthony's website: www.laurenceanth ony.net/software.html.

Figure 17 4-grams from the DDL corpus in AntConc

inseparable pair. Further exploration shows that *on the one hand* occurs 44 times in 34 papers, and without the determiner (*on one hand*) just 5 times in 3 papers; these are already potentially useful pedagogical findings. Glancing down the top 10 items, it surprises some to see so many determiners and prepositions (e.g. *the results of the, in the present study, in the form of*), which also highlights how these can be learned and used as chunks for more fluent writing (and reading). In ninth position, *in the case of* (119 occurrences in 62 files) can lead to comparison with *in case of*: just two occurrences which, in the KWIC tool (see Section 2), show a separate meaning (*in case of confusion / disagreement*); again, small words can make a difference in meaning, and the groups learned as chunks. The tenth item on this list may also surprise: *students were asked to*, where a grammatically equivalent structure would be impossible in French, for example (**les étudiants ont été demandés de*), which we would need to reformulate as something like 'we asked the students to' or 'it was asked of the students to'. Clicking on this takes the user straight to the KWIC tool to visualise the short occurrences in context; clicking on any of these opens the File View for the paper it is taken from. The Plot tool shows the number of times the phrase occurs in each paper, and where in that paper. This can be useful where particular items are associated with particular sections: *sample size*, for example, is most frequently found near the middle (the Methodology section) or the end (Conclusion, calling for larger studies in future).

If students want to identify specificities of their RA corpus, they can compare it against a reference corpus; this can either be a large, general collection such as the BNC (again, Anthony's website provides a wordlist for this, thus avoiding the need to load 100 million words!), which will bring out academic language as a whole, or perhaps another student's RA corpus in a different discipline for insights into the specific field. For this, the AntConc Keyword tool shows items that are significantly more frequent in one corpus than the other, though note that it does not show what they have in common. Sketch Engine provides easy access to many different corpora which can be used as reference corpora in a keyword analysis. Sketch Engine also gives users the chance to generate multi-word keyword terms, which is a convenient way to identify phrases that are specific to a corpus.

4.4.2 Writing Queries in ESAP

In several of these tools, clicking on an interactive item jumps automatically to the KWIC tool, but as we have seen throughout this Element, KWIC concordances can also be the starting point of a query to see words or phrases in context. For example, students may have been told that we do not use the first person (*I, me, we, our*, etc.) in academic writing. In our corpus above (1.2 m words, 191 papers: see 4.4.1), *we* occurs 2,143 times (1.7 per thousand words) in 152 papers (80 per cent), 35 of which use it over 20 times; of these though, all but one are co-authored papers. The KWIC tool orders hits by pattern, the most common with *we* being *we have seen* (12 occurrences); this suggests that *we* does not necessarily refer to the authors alone, but rather to the authors and readers together as a way of creating common ground. Other frequent verbs to the right (using the Collocate tool) include *believe, hope* and *expect*, which reflect the authors' stance; *propose* and *describe*, which serve to structure the paper; and *use* and *find*, which report on what happened (typically in the Methodology sections, as they occur rarely near the beginning or end of the papers). Similar searches can be conducted for *I*, complicated by the fact that it is often used as a number (*i*); the case-sensitive option can help with this. *I* can also be found in multi-authored papers: exploration shows that this is typically in extracts of student productions or feedback from questionnaires or interviews that occur in the text (long extracts were not included in the corpus). So the question of whether or not to use first-person pronouns is not as straightforward as some style guides suggest, though novice writers should certainly be careful in their use.

Returning to our earlier question about the term *amount* in COCA: a student may receive feedback that *large amounts of studies* sounds odd but not know quite why; searching for right collocates of *amount** in our corpus finds that most of the following nouns (*time, data, exposure, information, input, effort, training, practice*, etc.) are uncountable, which is indeed typical of *amount(s)* in COCA as well. The possible exception is *data*, which is notorious for soliciting strong but opposing views; the question is not whether it is 'really' countable or not, but how it is most typically used in the field we are attempting to enter. Left collocates include *these data* (f=29) more often than *this data* (17); to the right, *data were* (f=96), *was* (57), *is* (39) and *are* (38). So it seems that there is a slight preference in these articles published in visible international journals for plural, but both are possible.[46] The most important thing is perhaps to be consistent within a given paper.

4.4.3 Talking about Research and Results

Another issue lies in discussing tables and figures. To the right of the word *table* we find *shows* (f=160), *presents* (40), *summarizes* (34), *provides* (18), *illustrates* (16), and *displays* (12); to the right of *Figure*: *shows* (82) and *illustrates* (24). These suggest a number of common terms that are appropriate in our field and represent options for writers. While it is difficult to draw conclusions from negative evidence (i.e. what is not there) in a small corpus like this, French writers who may be tempted to write *in this Table we can see* might notice that there are no examples of this structure here. It would be perfectly grammatical, but it seems that English prefers to objectify the data source (*the Table shows*) rather than subjectifying the interpretation (*we can see*).

In a similar vein, reporting previous research is a main characteristic of RAs, but cultures may be different. The simplest way to see this with AntConc is to search for collocates of dates such as *19** or *20**.[47] This brings up both & (f=3184 to the left) and *and* (f=756). A quick perusal in KWIC format shows that the ampersand is (almost) exclusively used when citing a reference in brackets along with the date, separated by a comma, while the full form is in the main syntax of the sentence and the date only in brackets; compare the results in Figure 18. Studying the lines might show that in English (as opposed to, say, French), citations are more commonly relegated to brackets following an idea rather than starting a sentence – in English, the idea is more important than who said it. But we should not overgeneralise: the second structure is still frequently attested here, it is just less usual, so should be used parsimoniously for main topics. And when it is used, the corpus can provide examples of

---

[46] We have generally used it as singular / uncountable in this Element – an informed choice.

[47] There is a slight complication as this involves changing the tag settings when creating the corpus.

use of concordancers and corpora prior to their use (**Boulton & Cobb**, 2017; Götz & Mukherjee, 2006; McEnery & Wils	
). In particular, the results of recent meta-analyses (e.g. **Boulton & Cobb**, 2017; Lee, Warschauer, & Lee, 2019) paint a	
ade by the learners in other studies (Benavides, 2015; **Boulton & Cobb**, 2017; Liu & Jiang, 2009). Additionally, the positi	
derstand the role of DDL over other learning activities (**Boulton & Cobb**, 2017). Finally and most importantly, previous st	
litate their pattern induction in authentic language use (**Boulton & Cobb**, 2017). In view of Boulton's (2010) finding that	
What is more, the meta-analysis of 64 DDL studies by **Boulton and Cobb** (2017) reveals that hands-on tasks appear to	
2 learning approach. For example, based on 64 studies, **Boulton and Cobb** (2017) found that DDL was largely effective	
nion, & Morrison, 2018). Following Boulton (2010) and **Boulton and Cobb** (2017), the within-group comparisons were m	
to) exposure to instances of the construction. Since, as **Boulton and Cobb** (2017: 350) put it, "[r]ules are hard,	
as a 'medium' sample size for DDL studies according to **Boulton and Cobb** (2017). We have also already mentioned the	

Figure 18 Concordance extracts for *Boulton & Cobb* vs *Boulton and Cobb*

1.	ical approach where teacher instruction is mostly **didactic** or explanatory, the largely learner-centered direct DDL
2.	al context where instructors' instruction is mostly **didactic** or explanatory. Such a warning is noteworthy with res
3.	riting, correct errors and provide prescriptive and **didactic** advice to students about their language problems (Huii
4.	all Australian universities promote relatively non-**didactic** and student centred teaching practices which foster st
5.	d their US classmates) as a subsequent source of **didacticized** input (Swain & Lapkin, 1995). We further illustrat
6.	wide acceptability. The need was therefore for a "**didactic** language corpus" (Polezzi 1993) which could provide e
7.	nal aspects of learning from authentic rather than **didactic** material." (Mishan 2004, p. 219). The use of authentic
8.	ed alignment between DDL and language learning **didactics** (Meunier, 2019; Wicher, 2019). For example, Meunier
9.	oduction to the subject. It is academic writing in a **didactic** rather than a research context. A number of issues
10.	ould have been had the lesson been traditionally **didactically** taught" (p. 107) but defends this on the grounds th
11.	tagged corpus contains articles from Le Monde, a **didactic** text on the history and development of the French
12.	ir results support the idea that "AD is an excellent **didactic** tool to promote the four language skills (reading, writi

Figure 19 Full concordance for *didact** in 191 RAs

reporting verbs and other ways to integrate the citation into the sentence (*X found that, as X put it, the study by X reveals that, according to X*, etc.).

A corpus with a specific focus such as this can also be used for quite precise terminological considerations. It is a much simpler affair, for example, to see how *Data-Driven Learning* is referred to in the literature once all the literature has been collected and can be sorted and analysed through a tool like AntConc. More broadly, what is the difference between *pedagogical* and *didactic*? The first thing to notice is that the various forms of *pedagog** are about 100 times more frequent than *didact**, which has just 12 occurrences in 11 papers (Table 8). So the latter does exist, but is comparatively very rare. Is it possible to explain it? The complete list is provided in Figure 19, where several lines (1, 2, 3, 4, 10) suggest an almost pejorative definition of the word that corresponds more to traditional transmissive teaching, while others (5, 7, 11) contrast authentic materials with ones that have been adapted for teaching purposes. To take a different approach, we can ask who produced these texts. Some are quoted verbatim or indirectly from other sources, while many of the rest are from researchers who are familiar with French or other Romance languages through their place of work, mother tongue, or research and teaching practices. The upshot of all this is that in our field, the word family *didact** is probably best avoided altogether (see Miras et al., 2018, for a French take on this).

Table 8 *pedagog** and *didact** in 191 RAs

Rank	Type	Freq	Range	Norm Freq	Norm Range	Rank	Type	Freq	Range	Norm Freq	Norm Range
1	pedagogical	653	131	523.37	0.69	1	didactic	9	8	7.21	0.04
2	pedagogy	295	80	236.44	0.42	2	didactically	1	1	0.80	0.01
3	pedagogic	94	35	75.34	0.18	2	didacticized	1	1	0.80	0.01
4	pedagogically	68	41	54.50	0.22	2	didactics	1	1	0.80	0.01
5	pedagogies	14	7	11.22	0.04	**TOT**	**didact***	**12**	**11**	**9.62**	**0.06**
6	pedagogue(s)	3	3	2.40	0.02						
TOT	**pedagog***	**1127**	**157**	**903.28**	**0.82**						

4.5 Summary and Take-Home Message

This section has barely scratched the surface of what can be done using COCA or AntConc and other tools. Some are simple, some more complex; it is probably as well to use just one or two, and probably only a handful of features of each which are of most use to you. This is no different from other computer tools – millions of people use Microsoft Word on a daily basis without mastering the myriad different options. The same goes for building a corpus: it should be as big and clean as it needs to be, but diminishing returns mean that it is not worth spending vast amounts of time aiming at perfection. The section is certainly not a 'how-to' set of procedures even for these tools; in most cases, video tutorials can be found online (check for the latest version). Teachers can introduce the tools and approach in extremely controlled activities or entirely free exploration, or any-where between. With access to an appropriate corpus and minimal ability to use the chosen tool, the exploration procedure is very open. Sometimes there is a specific question which a student wants an answer to (Can I say this? What verb goes with this noun?); at other times the process is highly serendipitous, just opening the corpus and seeing what comes up, jumping from one tool and query to another, uncovering unexpected treasures in the process.

5 Data-Driven Learning in the Wild: Fostering Learner Autonomy

5.1 Introduction

As we have seen, DDL relies on noticing patterns in data to create knowledge (e.g. Boulton, 2021), and it does not really matter what type of data it is, corpora, language, or any other type of input from the world around us. Humans are good at seeing patterns – much better than they are than at understanding and applying rules, a complex intellectual activity (e.g. Jordan & Long, 2023). Patterns are also more realistic than formal rules, in that language is genuinely fuzzy and open to myriad variations, as indeed is much of our everyday experience of the world. In fact, we are so good at pattern-recognition that there is even a word – apophenia – for when we detect patterns that are not really there. Classic cases involve seeing a face in the clouds, or the Rohrschach tests used by psychologists, mere symmet-rical inkblots on a piece of paper. In the main, such 'type one errors' (false positives) are preferable to 'type two errors' (false negatives): for example, thinking that all dogs are dangerous even when they are not is more conducive to survival than thinking a species is harmless when it is not. Unfortunately, many superstitions and discriminatory stereotypes are also based on this natural tendency.

In our first language, most grammar and vocabulary is acquired from expos-ure to the language (listening or participating in conversation), almost by magic – it is virtually impossible not to acquire a 'mother tongue'. Exposure is also crucial in learning a new language later in life, often at school or university: research has shown that much L2 vocabulary is learned incidentally through exposure, especially via reading (the more the better; but see the exchange between Cobb et al., 2016). That said, by this stage we also have more advanced cognition and experience of the world to draw on, as well as our knowledge of our first language. This means we have options to consciously think about what we are learning and integrate it to existing knowledge (Schmidt, 1990).

Sometimes, though, we do not notice patterns in the world around us. We have all had the experience of encountering a new word or expression for the first time only to notice it repeatedly in the coming days, weeks or months; it seems likely we had actually met it before, but just had not noticed it until it came to our conscious attention. This is particularly the case when something is not salient in the input, and perhaps does not carry much meaning: many advanced learners say *discuss about*, even though this preposition does not occur after the verb in most of their input. And of course it would be logical: we have a *discussion about*, and say *talk about* – why not *discuss about*? Additionally, there may be a parallel structure in the learner's first language where an equivalent verb does have a preposition. It is also difficult to notice one thing when we are concentrating on something else; the famous 'invisible gorilla' experiment at Harvard[48] asked participants to count the number of passes made in a basketball match, which meant they did not see someone in a gorilla costume passing through the middle of the screen! In the case of language, if we focus only on the message, we may not notice the form; clearly some combination of the two is essential for communication and learning to take place at the same time.

An approach that builds on natural abilities is more likely to be taken up, fostering learner autonomy. Considerable research has been conducted on autonomy in language learning over the years, based on the precept that there are limits to the language the teacher can provide, so learners can usefully be encouraged to continue learning effectively on their own. This involves taking responsibility for decisions that are traditionally made by the teacher, such as what to learn, how, when, where, and so on. In this way, each learner can tailor their learning to their own specific needs and individual styles. A similar argument can be applied to the tools used: techniques that involve familiar, everyday tools are more likely to be retained. If we can show learners how to use them in just slightly new but more efficient ways, the benefits could be

---

[48] theinvisiblegorilla.com and https://shorturl.at/CVDTq. Once you know, it is difficult to imagine how you could have overlooked it.

considerable. This aligns with research in informal language learning, where learners are doing things spontaneously and of their own volition in another language, but where language itself is not the primary goal; obvious examples include watching TV series and videos on YouTube, reading and participating in social media, and so on. This section explores how these two aspects, autonomy and informal learning, can come together in DDL-like ways.

5.2 Everybody's Doing DDL

Precisely because interpreting and seeing patterns in data is natural, but not always easy, it should come as no surprise that people find ways to nudge themselves in the right direction for language. This might be as simple as highlighting words or phrases in a text, using colour, underlining, circles, and so on: such active reading practices are useful in themselves, and the items are made more salient when looking back (Szudarski & Carter, 2016). A teacher might write up two similar sentences on the blackboard (e.g. *she broke her arm / she's broken her arm*) and ask learners to discuss how the verb form contributes to making meaning. This clearly has little to do with DDL as we have presented it – using the tools and techniques of corpus linguistics to help L2 learning, but DDL builds on it. Other familiar, everyday tools can help as well, and though they do not involve a 'corpus' or a 'concordancer', they bring us closer to DDL by sorting data and making patterns more noticeable (Boulton, 2015). Among the simplest: if you have an electronic text, you can simply search for a word or phrase you encounter and see if it is repeated in that individual text – much easier than visually scanning a written text and highlighting the item (and involving less vandalism). The text in question might be a school textbook (for language or any other topic), a text that has been downloaded or written by the learner, or a webpage. For example, the word *data* occurs frequently on the Wikipedia page for statistics; as Figure 20 shows, simply searching (CTRL+F) highlights the word in context, revealing such patterns as *data analysis* and *data sets,* a *collection of data, statistical data, data drawn from, data are, to summarise data,* and so on, all of which are potentially relevant to someone needing to talk or write about this topic. Scrolling down the page will bring up more repetitions of the same, along with additional items.

Search engines such as Google provide another example of proto-DDL, that is, using computer tools to sort language data, though Google is not a corpus and its web downloads are not a corpus. It is important to remember that Google is designed to retrieve information, not language forms, and interprets the user's query as it sees fit. However, there are a number of filters available. The best known perhaps is the use of quotation marks to force Google to search for that

Two main statistical methods are used in **data** analysis: descriptive statistics, which summarize **data** from a sample using indexes such as the mean or standard deviation, and inferential statistics, which draw conclusions from **data** that are subject to random variation (e.g., observational errors, sampling variation).[4] Descriptive statistics are most often concerned with two sets of properties of a *distribution* (sample or population): *central tendency* (or *location*) seeks to characterize the distribution's central or typical value, while *dispersion* (or *variability*) characterizes the extent to which members of the distribution depart from its center and each other. Inferences made using mathematical statistics employ the framework of probability theory, which deals with the analysis of random phenomena.

A standard statistical procedure involves the collection of **data** leading to a test of the relationship between two statistical **data** sets, or a **data** set and synthetic **data** drawn from an idealized model. A hypothesis is proposed for the statistical relationship between the two **data** sets, an alternative to an idealized null hypothesis of no relationship between two **data** sets. Rejecting or disproving the null hypothesis is done using statistical tests that quantify the sense in which the null can be proven false, given the **data** that are used in the test. Working from a null hypothesis, two basic forms of error are recognized: Type I errors (null hypothesis is rejected when it is in fact true, giving a "false positive") and Type II errors (null hypothesis fails to be rejected when it is in fact false, giving a "false negative"). Multiple problems have come to be associated with this framework, ranging from obtaining a sufficient sample size to specifying an adequate null hypothesis.[4]

Figure 20 From Wikipedia: Statistics (11/02/24)

exact formulation and nothing else; when we do this, we can also use an asterisk (*) to indicate any word, just as with corpus searches; for example *"play a * role in"* can show adjectives that frequently occur in this context. Other options include *filetype:pdf* to exclude html texts such as blogs, or to use particular categories such as Google Scholar to focus the search. We can combine several of these to compare *"conduct research"* and *"conduct a research"* (note the inverted commas) in pdfs from Google Scholar (cf. Han & Shin, 2017). From Figure 21, we can see that both occur but that *conduct research* is much more frequent. Frequency alone is not always a reliable indicator, and we can treat the hits themselves as short contexts not vastly dissimilar to a concordance: for this it is best to look at quite a few occurrences for patterns to emerge, and perhaps not to take the first few pages of hits. But with just these short samples, we can see that *a research* is usually followed by another noun: *a research plan, a research project, a research study.* In other words, it is not *a research* but *a [research] plan, a [research] project, a [research] study*; *research* is usually uncountable.

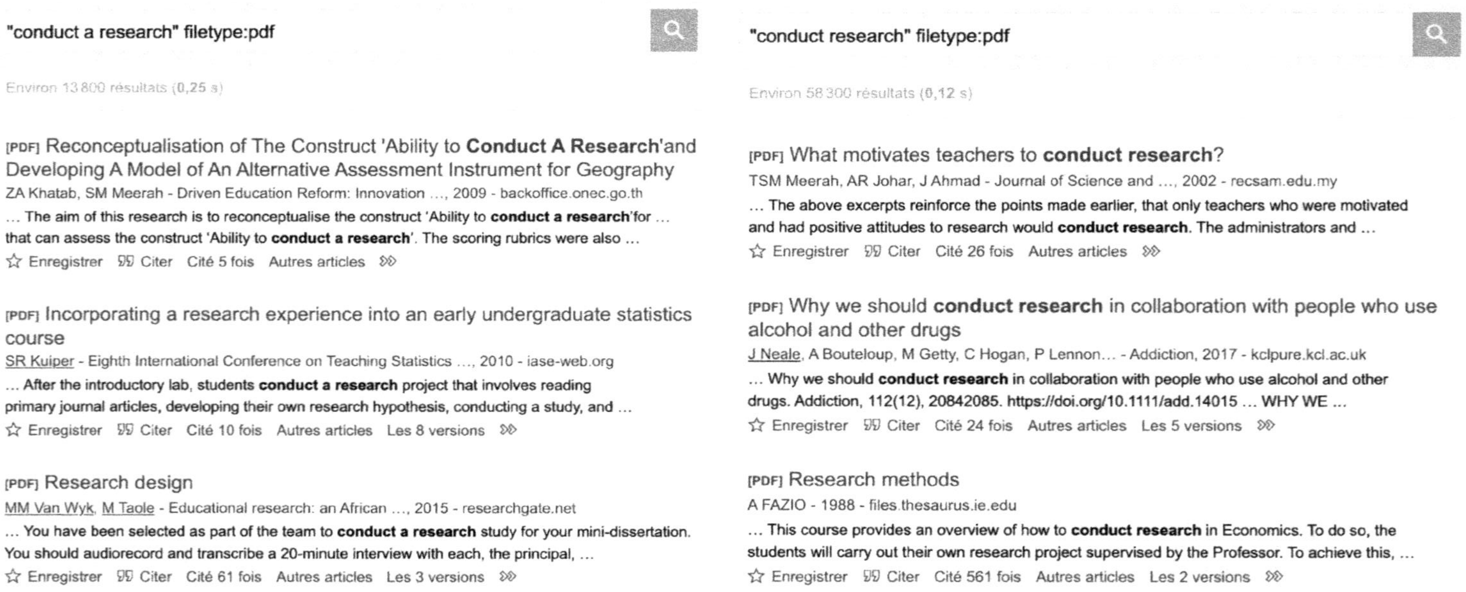

Figure 21 Comparing *conduct a research* and *conduct research* (11/02/24)

An example of how such techniques can engage autonomy and informal learning is provided in Gatto (2019), who worked with a group of twenty-two secondary-school students (see Section 3) aged 15 to 17 in the south of Italy. The students were invited to carry out a range of searches, refining their queries in an iterative process where they gained confidence in their interpretation of the results. As a warm-up activity, students were asked to search for *accomodation* and *accommodation* and observe the number of hits, and interpret the reliability of the web as a linguistic resource. After this, they were asked to explore collocations for a variety of words, which facilitated a discussion about the use of inverted commas (" ") in searches and the interpretation of linguistic evidence on the web. Gatto developed her own worksheets to be completed by the students while making sense of the information found on the internet. These worksheets helped the students focus on the task and think about the role of frequency and the methods used to extract information from the internet. Other activities included the use of translation candidates and expanded complex searches. While web searches differ from interactions with corpus interfaces, Gatto shows how quantitative findings from Google searches can create the conditions for conversations with secondary-school students where they can learn to support their learning with 'Data-Driven solutions to problems concerning language usage' (p. 121). In these activities, the learners engaged with the interpretation of the results provided by Google. The impact of alternative search options to Google and the like needs some attention, but the basic message is that such techniques are readily mastered and can be pursued autonomously after minimal training.

Google is constantly evolving though, along with the data on its servers, and adapts results to each user's history, so teachers should be careful not to expect exactly the same results each time. And as it is essentially a black box in terms of both contents and algorithms, it is important to be critical in examining the results. The point is that our learners today are familiar with such tools, whereas in the early days of DDL there was no internet, no windows, and some learners were introduced to hands-on corpus work without ever having even used a computer keyboard. Many learners are likely already using Google in the way outlined above; perhaps we can help them do it better. That would already be a step forward, and may be enough for some; for others, such familiar tools may represent a relatively painless introduction to the principles of DDL – using computer tools to query and sort language data.

5.3 Scenario 1: DDL without a Corpus

One possible objection with many corpora is that the language is too advanced for the learners. Some simpler corpora do exist, such as the graded readers or

Simple Wikipedia texts on Tom Cobb's LexTutor[49] website: just select 'from corpus' to see the range on offer. An alternative is to choose texts that learners can relate to (Section 3). This might be a set of documents from their coursework, their own writing, scripts from films of TV series that they know, and so on; many such texts can be found online, from official websites or fan transcripts (which might need some checking). By being involved and working with familiar texts, learners may achieve a greater sense of 'ownership', with results that are meaningful and produce a sense of satisfaction from understanding authentic language on their own. In his final publication, Tim Johns et al. (2008) worked with the *Swallows and Amazons* books from his favourite writer with school-aged students in Taiwan. The book was assigned reading, one section per week, which the learners found highly motivating, as well as benefiting from being able to query each section in the software. Clearly a novel is not a 'corpus', but even a single long text can be used with corpus software, the topic of the next section.

5.3.1 A Corpus Starts with a Single Text

Many well-known novels and other texts are no longer subject to copyright and can be downloaded from repositories such as Project Gutenberg[50] already in txt format. We have chosen *Alice's Adventures in Wonderland* by Lewis Carrol; though written in 1865, the language is generally quite accessible, and many learners will have the advantage of having watched one of the several films based on it, meaning they already have useful expectations. With very little work to remove the boilerplate and save sections separately, this gives us a small 'corpus' of under 30,000 words in 12 sections. For a teacher choosing a text, corpus tools can help with assessing difficulty. Going via COCA[51] on Mark Davies' website (see Section 2): choose the icon at the top that looks like a page of text (), copy section 1 of *Alice* and paste it into the window, then click 'analyse text'. For the sake of clarity, Figure 22 shows the results for just the first five paragraphs: very common words range from 1 to 500 (70%) (among the 500 most frequent words in English), mid-range words range from 501 to 3000 (9%) (within the top 3000 items), less frequent items indicated as >3000 (10%); grey is mainly for capitalised words which we can ignore for the moment. The words are grouped into bands on the right, by frequency. Such information can help the teacher to decide if the text is at the appropriate level for their students,

---

[49] LexTutor concordancing: www.lextutor.ca/conc/eng.
[50] Project Gutenberg: www.gutenberg.org.
[51] Corpus of Contemporary American English: www.english-corpora.org/coca.

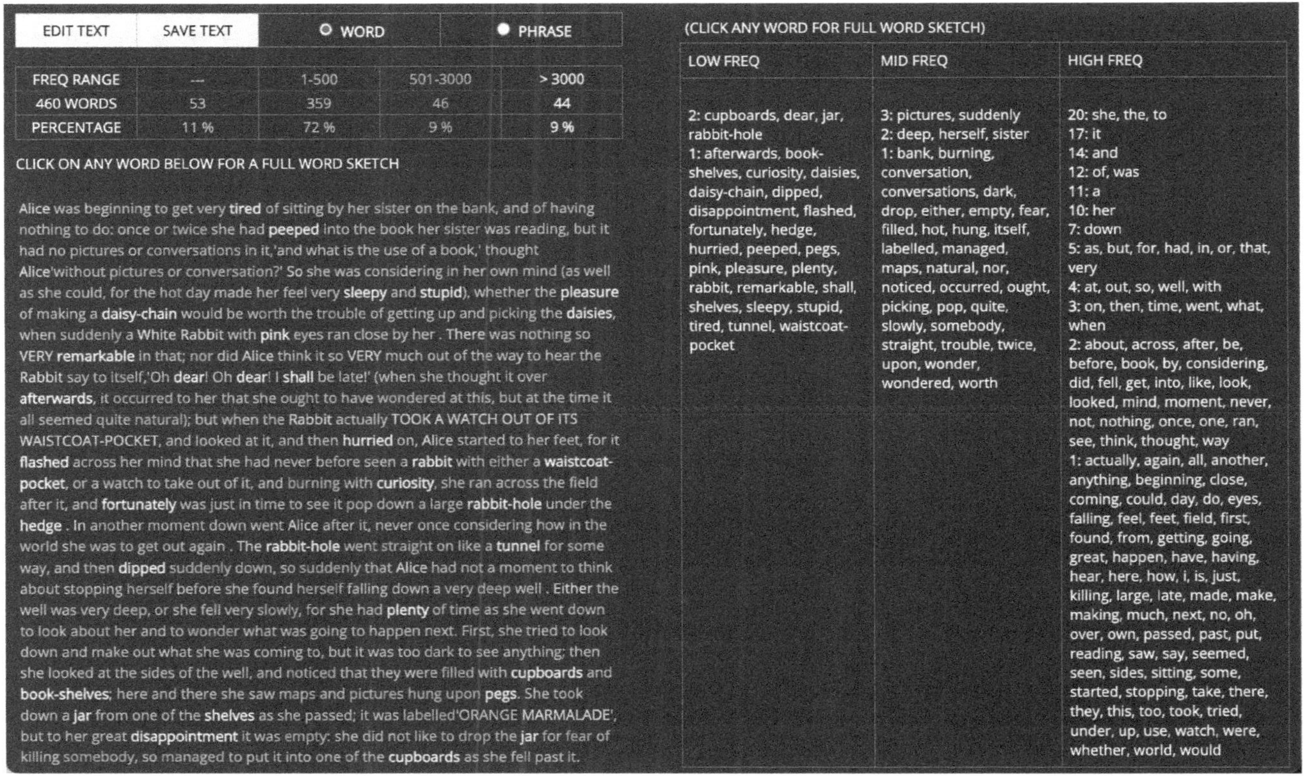

EDIT TEXT	SAVE TEXT	○ WORD	● PHRASE

FREQ RANGE	—	1-500	501-3000	> 3000
460 WORDS	53	359	46	44
PERCENTAGE	11 %	72 %	9 %	9 %

CLICK ON ANY WORD BELOW FOR A FULL WORD SKETCH

Alice was beginning to get very **tired** of sitting by her sister on the bank, and of having nothing to do: once or twice she had **peeped** into the book her sister was reading, but it had no pictures or conversations in it,'and what is the use of a book,' thought Alice'without pictures or conversation?' So she was considering in her own mind (as well as she could, for the hot day made her feel very **sleepy** and **stupid**), whether the **pleasure** of making a **daisy-chain** would be worth the trouble of getting up and picking the **daisies**, when suddenly a White Rabbit with **pink** eyes ran close by her . There was nothing so VERY **remarkable** in that; nor did Alice think it so VERY much out of the way to hear the Rabbit say to itself,'Oh **dear**! Oh **dear**! I **shall** be late!' (when she thought it over **afterwards**, it occurred to her that she ought to have wondered at this, but at the time it all seemed quite natural); but when the Rabbit actually TOOK A WATCH OUT OF ITS WAISTCOAT-POCKET, and looked at it, and then **hurried** on, Alice started to her feet, for it **flashed** across her mind that she had never before seen a **rabbit** with either a **waistcoat-pocket**, or a watch to take out of it, and burning with **curiosity**, she ran across the field after it, and **fortunately** was just in time to see it pop down a large **rabbit-hole** under the **hedge** . In another moment down went Alice after it, never once considering how in the world she was to get out again . The **rabbit-hole** went straight on like a **tunnel** for some way, and then **dipped** suddenly down, so suddenly that Alice had not a moment to think about stopping herself before she found herself falling down a very deep well . Either the well was very deep, or she fell very slowly, for she had **plenty** of time as she went down to look about her and to wonder what was going to happen next. First, she tried to look down and make out what she was coming to, but it was too dark to see anything; then she looked at the sides of the well, and noticed that they were filled with **cupboards** and **book-shelves**; here and there she saw maps and pictures hung upon **pegs**. She took down a **jar** from one of the **shelves** as she passed; it was labelled'ORANGE MARMALADE', but to her great **disappointment** it was empty: she did not like to drop the **jar** for fear of killing somebody, so managed to put it into one of the **cupboards** as she fell past it.

(CLICK ANY WORD FOR FULL WORD SKETCH)

LOW FREQ	MID FREQ	HIGH FREQ
2: cupboards, dear, jar, rabbit-hole 1: afterwards, book-shelves, curiosity, daisies, daisy-chain, dipped, disappointment, flashed, fortunately, hedge, hurried, peeped, pegs, pink, pleasure, plenty, rabbit, remarkable, shall, shelves, sleepy, stupid, tired, tunnel, waistcoat-pocket	3: pictures, suddenly 2: deep, herself, sister 1: bank, burning, conversation, conversations, dark, drop, either, empty, fear, filled, hot, hung, itself, labelled, managed, maps, natural, nor, noticed, occurred, ought, picking, pop, quite, slowly, somebody, straight, trouble, twice, upon, wonder, wondered, worth	20: she, the, to 17: it 14: and 12: of, was 11: a 10: her 7: down 5: as, but, for, had, in, or, that, very 4: at, out, so, well, with 3: on, then, time, went, what, when 2: about, across, after, be, before, book, by, considering, did, fell, get, into, like, look, looked, mind, moment, never, not, nothing, once, one, ran, see, think, thought, way 1: actually, again, all, another, anything, beginning, close, coming, could, day, do, eyes, falling, feel, feet, field, first, found, from, getting, going, great, happen, have, having, hear, here, how, i, is, just, killing, large, late, made, make, making, much, next, no, oh, over, own, passed, past, put, reading, saw, say, seemed, seen, sides, sitting, some, started, stopping, take, there, they, this, too, took, tried, under, up, use, watch, were, whether, world, would

Figure 22 COCA analysis of *Alice's Adventures in Wonderland*

Figure 23 COCA information for *hurried*

if certain items might benefit from pre-teaching or inferring from context, and so on.

Davies was not the first to create this type of tool, and several others can be found online, along with rationales for word bands and word families (e.g. Laufer & Cobb, 2020). But the advantage here is that it is possible to go further by clicking on a single word such as *hurried*, which occurs on the first page of the novel.[52] This takes us to a new page (Figure 23) with tremendous amounts of information about this word: we can see that it is a verb here, the bars top left showing that it is particularly frequent in TV/Movie language and Fiction. This is followed by a definition and links to external websites for further research, then synonyms and, on the right, information about the context, collocates and related words. Lower down we have clusters for the different forms of the verb, and KWIC concordances for short contexts (just 10 are given here). All of this can be of help to the teacher in planning how to teach the word, or to have learners explore autonomously as and when the need arises. All of this corpus information has been obtained without conducting a corpus query.

---

[52] Similar information can be obtained for any word or phrase search, by using the 'word' tab on the query page. For more information, see www.youtube.com/watch?v=ryC2gYPO8fk.

ıe came trotting along in a great	hurry,	muttering to himself as he came,	ɔng the party. Some of the birds	hurried	off at once: one old Magpie beg
n't indeed!' said Alice, in a great	hurry	to change the subject of conversa	ɔok up the little golden key and	hurried	off to the garden door. Poor Alic
ead made her look up in a great	hurry.	An enormous puppy was looking	the moment they saw her, they	hurried	back to the game, the Queen mɛ
' the Dormouse began in a great	hurry '	and their names were Elsie, Lacie,	ɟ at her feet as the White Rabbit	hurried	by--the frightened Mouse splas
larch Hare interrupted in a great	hurry. '	You did!' said the Hatter. 'I deny i	White Rabbit: it was talking in a	hurried	nervous manner, smiling at ever
te Rabbit, jumping up in a great	hurry: '	this paper has just been picked u	and, taking Alice by the hand, it	hurried	off, without waiting for the end
you do lessons?' said Alice, in a	hurry	to change the subject. 'Ten hours	f,' said the King eagerly, and he	hurried	off. Alice thought she might as v
rp hiss made her draw back in a	hurry	a large pigeon had flown into her	:KET, and looked at it, and then	hurried	on, Alice started to her feet, for
ɛ was not going to do THAT in a	hurry. '	No, I'll look first,' she said, 'and s	·oquet with the Queen,' and she	hurried	out of the room. The cook threw
ɛs, and she jumped up in such a	hurry	that she tipped over the jury–box	Hush!' said the Rabbit in a low,	hurried	tone. He looked anxiously over l
d tumbled head over heels in its	hurry	to get hold of it; then Alice, think	ɛ went in without knocking, and	hurried	upstairs, in great fear lest she sl

Figure 24 AntConc contexts for *hurry* and *hurried*, sorted left and right respectively

The examples above take us outside the novel, but we can remain on-target by loading our text into AntConc, just as we would with a corpus. The Word function shows that *hurry* and *hurried* each occur 11 times in the book (along with two occurrences of *hurriedly* and one of *hurrying*), which we can then look at to see how they are used in the book (see e.g. Hadley & Charles, 2017). Figure 24 shows that the form *hurry* is usually a noun, and occurs mainly in the phrase *in a hurry*; it is possible to add an adjective (*in a great hurry*) or to change the determiner (*in its hurry*), but the pattern is much clearer than it would have been without the tool to sort the data. Similarly, *hurried* is usually a verb, and is always followed by an adverb particle here (*off, back, by, on, out, upstairs*); in the two seeming exceptions, *hurried* is an adjective followed by a noun (*a hurried nervous manner*; *a low, hurried tone*). Of course, this is not a complete description of *hurry* or *hurried*, but the key advantage lies in seeing how it is used in this Element precisely without being distracted by other possibilities. These can always be added later if and when the time comes.

Online tools like the English Vocabulary Profile or the English Grammar Profile,[53] both based on the Cambridge Learner Corpus, provide complementary information and further context to how language learners use vocabulary and grammar across the Common European Framework of Reference for Languages (CEFR) competence levels. In our case, these online tools can contextualise the different senses of *hurry* from A2 to B2, both as a noun and as a verb, providing a link between uses of the word and its attested uses in learner corpus data. More specifically, it is of course possible for a teacher to create a corpus of their own learners' language use, typically for writing and useful for error correction or simply noticing the gap – features that contrast between the learners and some target. This might be experts, for example in published research articles (see Section 4), or L1 students with similar profiles (e.g. in MICUSP or BAWE). Though such learner corpora can be

---

[53] www.englishprofile.org.

quite time-consuming to compile at the start, once created they can be used for several years, updated as and when necessary.

5.3.2 GenAI and DDL

The arrival of the GenAI tool ChatGPT in November 2022 has engendered tremendous debate in education as in other areas, but much tends to be a knee-jerk reaction at opposite ends of the spectrum: GenAI is neither the end of the world nor the solution to all our problems. It is certainly true that it has much to offer language users and learners, but like any tool, it is better at some things than others, and is not always the best choice. First though, an example of the type of thing that can be done with GenAI, more specifically OpenAI's ChatGPT as this is still the best-known free AI Chatbot. Others such as Google's Gemini or Microsoft's Copilot may prove to be market leaders, or indeed any one of a number of others provided by major companies or start-ups. As we have seen, a major function of DDL is to provide collocation information and examples in context. Students can now do the same thing with ChatGPT. One main advantage is that the question can be asked in ordinary language, with no need to master a concordancer or how to formulate queries, which may require several iterations. The output in Figure 25 was the result of two queries: 'What words collocate with *rain*?' Followed by: 'Can you provide an example of use, the type of text where the example is used and the relative frequencies of the collocates provided?'

The collocates in Figure 25 represent a mix of different types (weather reports and casual conversations), which may be confusing for language learners, and because we do not know how the results were obtained, we may be sceptical of the frequency notes. Authenticity is another issue. When asked if they were actual examples if they had been made up, ChatGPT responded: 'The examples provided were created for illustrative purposes and are not directly taken from a corpus. However, they are representative of typical usage based on the collocates provided.' It continued: 'If you need actual examples from a corpus, tools like the British National Corpus (BNC) or Corpus of Contemporary American English (COCA) can be used to extract authentic sentences. Would you like me to provide actual corpus-based examples?' We then asked for this, but ChatGPT returned invented examples even though we explicitly asked it not to make anything up. It subsequently apologised for the 'error', but despite repeated requests, it continued to hallucinate, providing examples which it incorrectly claimed were taken directly from COCA.

It is beyond the scope of this Element to provide a comprehensive survey of early research on GenAI, but several papers have explicitly explored the

1. **Heavy rain:**
   - Example: "The road was flooded due to heavy rain."
   - Type of text: Weather forecast, news report.
   - Relative frequency: High. Heavy rain is a common term used to describe intense precipitation.
2. **Light rain:**
   - Example: "We decided to go for a walk despite the light rain."
   - Type of text: Casual conversation, weather forecast.
   - Relative frequency: Moderate. Light rain is a commonly used term to describe gentle precipitation.
3. **Rain showers:**
   - Example: "The forecast predicts scattered rain showers throughout the afternoon."
   - Type of text: Weather forecast, news report.
   - Relative frequency: Moderate. Rain showers are a common weather phenomenon, especially in certain seasons.
4. **Torrential rain:**
   - Example: "The city experienced torrential rain, causing widespread flooding."
   - Type of text: News report, weather warning.
   - Relative frequency: Moderate. Torrential rain is used to describe very heavy rainfall, often associated with severe weather events.
5. **Drizzling rain:**
   - Example: "We walked in the park under the drizzling rain, enjoying the quiet atmosphere."
   - Type of text: Descriptive narrative, casual conversation.
   - Relative frequency: Moderate. Drizzling rain is a term used to describe very light, fine rain.

Figure 25 ChatGPT 3.5[54] list of collocates of *rain*

relationship between GenAI and DDL. One early advocate is Lin (2023), though she needed to write instructions running to nearly 1000 words for ChatGPT to simulate a corpus search exactly how she wanted. Repeating her procedures with our own search terms, we found the results to be less than perfect, with some not being what we asked for, others sounding very artificial or containing significant errors. However, GenAI will no doubt improve as it evolves. John Flowerdew is another enthusiast, finding that many of the tasks he gave in DDL workshops can be replicated, to an extent, with GenAI tools. He concludes however that 'there is still a place for DDL as we know it,' with 'the answer [lying] in a synthesis of both approaches' (p. 17). Crosthwaite and Baisa (2023) take a more balanced approach in exploring the relative merits of GenAI and corpora, arguing that each has something to offer. In other words, we should play to the strengths of each, using

---

[54] ChatGPT 4o returned similar, vague results, claiming that the results offered were based on 'insights on relative frequencies based on corpus data (e.g., the British National Corpus or Corpus of Contemporary American English)'. No details about frequencies, absolute or normalised, were provided.

DDL when it is most useful, and GenAI when that is (see also Mizumoto, 2023). This is reminiscent of an earlier debate about whether DDL teachers should still use dictionaries: the answer of course is to use it when it is the best tool available. We feel strongly that we should not force GenAI to imitate DDL, since we already have the tools for DDL and the imitation is a poor copy; GenAI should be used for other things where it can do what DDL cannot. Another objection to GenAI is that it does not help with learning *per se*, which again reflects an earlier concern of Tim Johns (1986, p. 156) for DDL tools: 'There is the pedagogic danger that one may, by making the program more powerful, be giving the machine tasks to do that should be left to the learner.' Of course, if you simply ask ChatGPT to produce a text, then the focus is entirely on the finished product. But students can also ask it to correct or comment their own texts, indicate errors along with suggested corrections or usage notes. This involves the learner in being critical about the information provided, just as they should be with teacher corrections and comments – and just as they are with DDL. Learning can then take place. GenAI may also be able to help with interpreting corpus results, and Anthony has integrated it into AntConc v4 for this very purpose.

So while it is tempting to use GenAI chatbots as easy-to-query corpus substitutes, they are by no means the same thing. Applications of GenAI Chatbots and corpora are structured differently and serve different purposes. Table 9 offers a breakdown of these differences.

The speed with which new applications for existing LLMs are appearing, as well as the pace at which new models are spreading, makes it virtually impossible to generalise about the future range of applications of these models to language education. One positive trend is the emergence of LLMs that can run on local machines and therefore allow for greater privacy when sharing data with external servers. Similarly, the application of LLMs in specific domains and tailored to the needs of specific user groups such as language learners will be a breakthrough soon. To conclude, GenAI does seem to present 'revolutionary opportunities and challenges for corpus applications to language learning' (Flowerdew, 2024, p. 1), but the technology is still too recent and evolving too fast for a definitive take. It is simply too early to say. Learners are perhaps best served by being introduced to the different tools currently available, and equipped with the know-how to check potential and pitfalls for different uses so that they can make their own decisions in future as things develop.

5.4 Scenario 2: DDL for Spoken Language

Most corpora involve only written text which is comparatively easy to collect and to analyse, but much teaching focuses on spoken language. Recording and

Table 9 Some differences between corpora and LLMs

GenAI Chatbots	Corpora + Concordancers
LLMs are pretrained general purpose language models that perform tasks such as text summarisation, question answering, text classification, and text generation.	Corpora are compiled and tools designed specifically for analysis of language use, and visual presentations to help with this.
Queries can be formulated in everyday language and entirely open-ended, but sometimes have to be very long to obtain the desired result.	The tools can only perform certain functions which have to be mastered, but once acquired, this makes the procedures much faster.
Search results are quick to obtain but users are in the dark when it comes to the evaluation of the exact sources used and the scope of the textual data that was analysed to return the specific results on the screen.	Corpora and corpus tools facilitate search results that are transparent and repeatable.
Size wise, LLMs are huge datasets. Some of them are measured in petabytes (1 pb = 1,000,000 gigabytes). The user can ask for results to be tailored to specific language varieties or learner profiles. It is also possible to create custom GPTs.[55]	Although some of the corpora from the enTenTen family on Sketch Engine are now beyond 50 billion words, the value of a corpus is not measured against its size, but rather against its ability to represent language use across contexts of use. Different corpora are required for different text types or needs, whether found or created.
The output from conversation agents such as ChatGPT may hallucinate, contain errors or misleading results.	Results from corpora can only contain language that has been used in real contexts of use and, so far, generated by humans.
Some tools are free, but only the paying ones guarantee that uploaded data is not stored or reused for undeclared purposes.	Some tools are paying, but to the best of our knowledge user data and uploaded texts do not give rise to ethical concerns.

---

[55] See e.g. the video tutorial at www.youtube.com/watch?v=5c3VRE5_hhc.

transcribing speech is expensive and time-consuming if done well, and presents a number of difficulties in searching (e.g. do you look for *do not know, don't know,* or *dunno*?). One of the largest sets of readily available transcripts can be found by searching in the 'spoken' section of COCA; this is mostly taken from online sources (relatively unscripted TV and radio programmes automatically transcribed) which have their imperfections but, as Mark Davies has said, it is much better than nothing. Others include the BNC, more carefully collected and based on a demographically representative sample of people who were paid to record their conversations over several weeks, all then manually transcribed. This is hugely expensive to do on a large scale, so many spoken corpora are more focused, such as MICASE[56] for American and BASE[57] as a near-equivalent for British English academic speech. Some useful filters mean it is possible to search MICASE by speaker (gender, age, position, first language) and by context (type of speech event, discipline, interactivity) – though the corpus being quite small, too many filters may give too few results to be of use (see e.g. Nergis, 2021).

5.4.1 TED Talks as a Source for Spoken Language

The spoken corpora mentioned above are however still 'written', in the sense that there is no sound or video. Speech corpora do exist but come with difficulties of their own (e.g. Chen & Tian, 2022). With written text, the KWIC format makes it easy to visualise many short extracts at once, where we clearly cannot listen to lots of voices at the same time. However, that does not mean it is entirely impossible, and some corpora exist with text and sound/video aligned. One example of this is from Yoichiro Hasebe, who created a corpus of TED talks[58] – presentations by experts on a wide variety of topics intended to stimulate an adult but non-specialist audience (see Section 3). The topics are serious, and the delivery usually clear and supported by a slideshow, but presentations may not be representative of interactive communication. The user can type in a word or phrase and see examples in KWIC format; clicking on the 'play video' button for one of these opens the video at the right point, but it is necessary to select each context individually; rolling subtitles are available below, often with a translation on the right. Figure 26 shows the example of *know what I mean,* which in context may appear in the frames *you know . . .* or *do you know . . .* or *if you know . . .* at the front, with varying intonations that learners can explore to compare meanings. Many teachers already ask their

---

[56] Michigan Corpus of Academic Spoken English: https://quod.lib.umich.edu/cgi/c/corpus/corpus?c=micase.

[57] British Academic Spoken English corpus: https://www.coventry.ac.uk/research/research-directories/current-projects/2015/british-academic-spoken-english-corpus-base/search-the-base-corpus/.

[58] TED Corpus Search Engine: http://yohasebe.com/tcse.

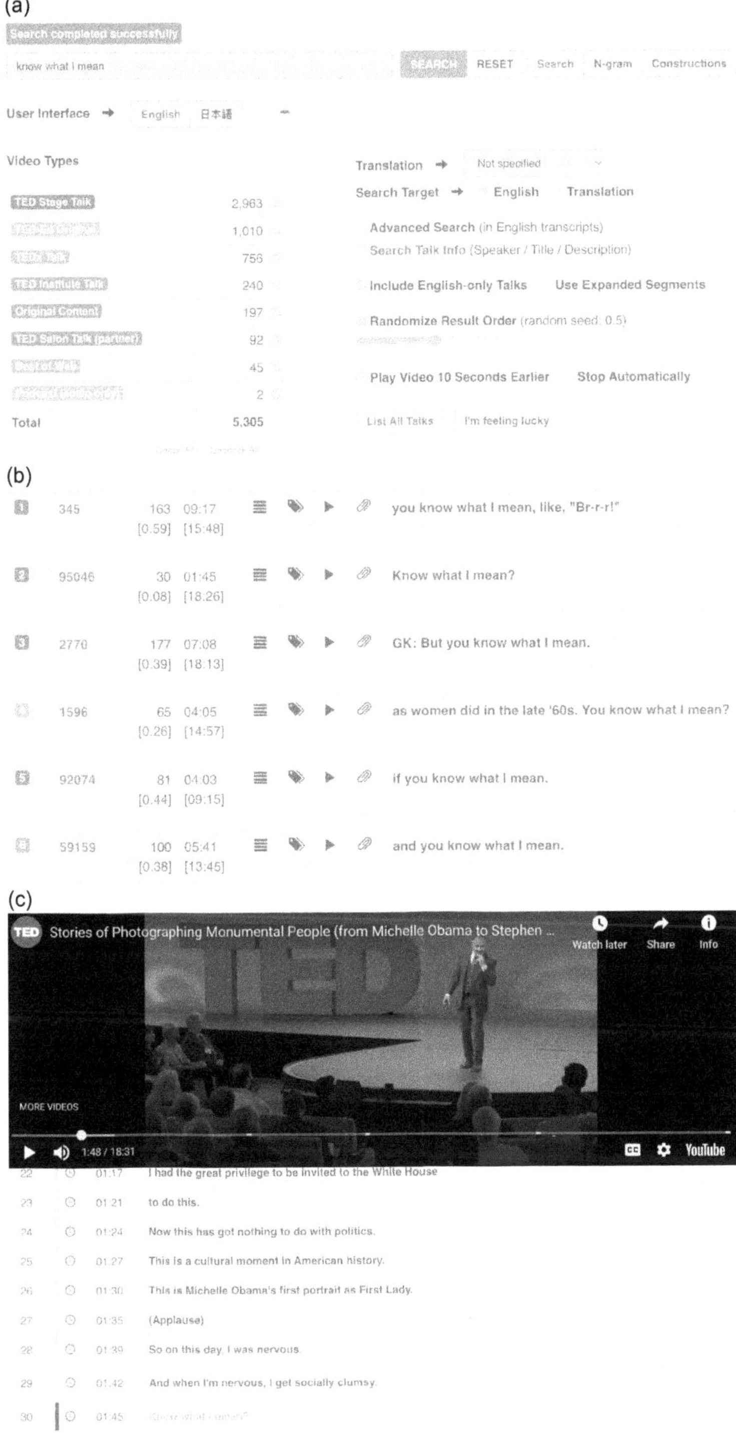

Figure 26 TCSE presentation for *know what I mean*: (a) query interface; (b) results from different videos; (c) extract with rolling transcription

students to watch specific videos; being able to explore language features within similar contexts represents only a small addition to the workload but has the potential to increase learners' investment as they choose the items that interest them. And an interesting clip may lead them to watch more videos autonomously.

5.4.2 General Tools for Spoken DDL

Another useful website is PlayPhrase,[59] a collection of films and TV series which have the added advantage that learners may see actors and actresses they recognise, and of course hear the original voices. But teachers beware: such videos are more likely to include taboo words or topics that may be inappropriate for younger learners. Typing in a word or phrase will take them to several occurrences which play automatically one after the other; the free version limits this to just five hits per query but these can be replayed, and any new query gives another five hits. The interface allows for fewer options than most such tools. Figure 27 shows one of the results for *idea* which French learners typically pronounce like *I.D.* /aidi:/. And we can go beyond just word pronunciation: in the five videos, we can see and hear groups of words including *do you have any idea . . ., very bad idea, I have an idea, I had no idea*, each of which can be used as the focus of collective reflection on pronunciation of the word *idea* in context,

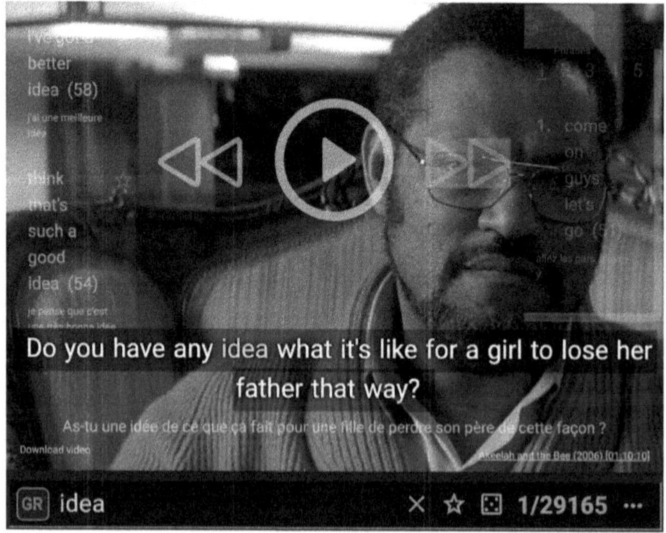

Figure 27 PlayPhrase presentation for *idea*

---

[59] PlayPhrase: https://playphrase.me.

and lead to further searches for these longer phrases – some suggestions including the target word appear on screen when it is paused.

YouGlish operates on a similar principle to PlayPhrase, taking subtitled videos found online, but rather than films or TV series, the samples are from YouTube, giving a wider variety of situations (Fu & Yang, 2019). The site also works with a number of languages, and for English we can choose between American, British, and Australian accents (the algorithms are not entirely accurate, so it may be useful to listen to several occurrences). It can also be incorporated into the teacher's own web platform with no adverts. Type in a word or phrase and again it takes the user automatically to the appropriate point of the first video, just a few seconds before the target item; each video plays until clicking the 'next' button, and can be slowed down or speeded up. Further information can be found on the same page, including definitions of each word in the subtitle, along with a phonetic transcription. The tool can be used for vocabulary, expressions, and pronunciation practice, observing how words or phrases are used in context. For example, the so-called 'quotative like' is a use of the word *like* to express what someone says or how they react in a conversational narrative. Using *I was like* brings up a series of occurrences, each with subtitles (Figure 28). What is important here is that, in this sense, it is

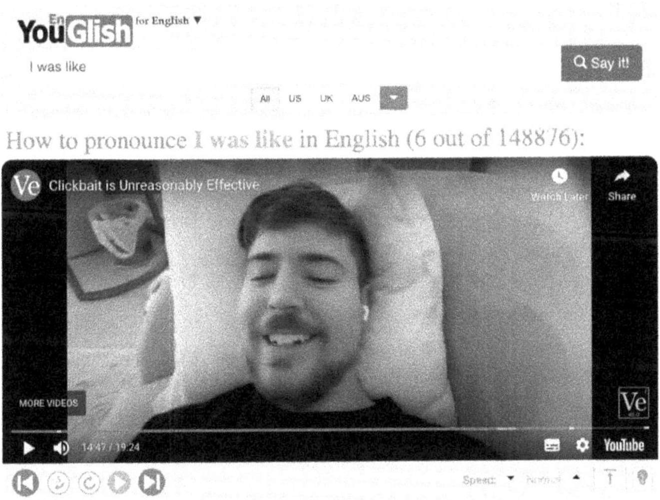

Figure 28 YouGlish presentation for *I was like*

almost a fixed expression, with a meaning that cannot necessarily be worked out from the individual words; context can help to understand this. In fact, it is such a fixed phrase that the words slide together – in extreme cases almost sounding like a single syllable, '*slike*'.

5.5 Summary and Take-Home Message

The point of this section has been to show that 'everybody's doing DDL', or at least things that have parallels in DDL. Adopting DDL practices should not mean making learning arduous and technical, and 'DDL-lite' can help learners be more effective in practices they already employ, becoming more autonomous in their exploration of language in informal contexts. In other words, rather than expecting a lot from learners and having them make the journey towards DDL, DDL-lite may provide a way to bring the essentials to them. It also seems likely that such ordinary, everyday, familiar tools that are already frequently used will continue to be consulted, reducing the chances they will be forgotten at the end of the course. For some, improvements in their current uses will already represent a relatively major return on a small investment; for others, it may provide a springboard to more prototypical DDL – it all depends on their circumstances and motivation. There is no single 'right' way to do DDL.

6 Take-Away Messages and Future Developments

Data-Driven Learning (DDL) emphasises an inductive, learner-centred approach that encourages autonomy, critical thinking, and awareness of language patterns. In DDL activities, language learners explore real-world texts, which helps them develop language skills applicable across a range of settings. This Element has discussed some topics that are central to present and future language learning in digital contexts where DDL can play an important role. Let us review these topics.

Empowering learners through autonomy and discovery
DDL shifts the focus from rule-based, often prescriptive teaching to an approach where learners explore language independently or with the guidance of their teachers. This encourages deeper engagement as learners notice patterns on their own and construct their own knowledge.

Adapting tools and techniques for diverse contexts
The versatility of DDL has been demonstrated across different educational settings, from schools to universities. Tools like concordancers and pedagogic corpora can be adapted to fit the specific needs of different groups of language learners; and many general, familiar tools such as Google can be used in DDL-like ways.

Integration of technology and traditional methods
The development of DDL tools such as AntConc and Sketch Engine provides language learners with practical ways to explore language in conjunction with more traditional learning methods. If teachers facilitate this integration, DDL activities will become purposeful and aligned with their students' learning objectives.

Focus on real-world language usage
By working with authentic language data, including collocations and genre-specific features, DDL helps learners understand language as it is actually used, rather than relying solely on textbook examples or dictionary definitions which may not be representative, or not relevant to their particular needs.

Language learning in the digital age
With the rise of generative AI and large language models, DDL's principles remain important for fostering digital literacy and a critical understanding of language data. Analysing real language examples will be crucial in the increasingly digital educational environment.

DDL present and future
DDL represents a forward-thinking approach to language teaching that offers both teachers and learners powerful tools for exploring and understanding language use. This Element has underscored the potential of DDL to make learning more engaging and data-informed in diverse educational contexts. As GenAI continues to evolve, DDL will be central to understanding how AI-generated content can impact language learning. By using DDL frameworks, educators can teach learners to evaluate AI-generated language critically, comparing it to authentic language data to identify discrepancies, biases, or, among others, non-standard usages.

The focus of DDL on data analysis and pattern recognition provides language learners with skills to evaluate both language patterns and AI-generated materials, ensuring they develop a good understanding of both human and machine-generated language. This integration will foster not only language proficiency but also the critical digital literacy required in modern, digital educational contexts. This type of literacy will most certainly be key in the forthcoming future.

Glossary

Academic purposes: Teaching languages for the purpose of using them in academic contexts – at university, or for presentations or writing (ERPP: English for Research Publication Purposes), etc.

Annotation: In corpus linguistics, annotation is information that is added to a text in a given corpus; most frequently for part of speech, but also for grammatical role, meaning, etc.

AntConc: Multiplatform, free-to-use desktop corpus management software. www.laurenceanthony.net/software/antconc.

BNC | the British National Corpus: A 100-million word corpus of British English originally released in the early 1990s; a new spoken 10-million word dataset is available. www.english-corpora.org/bnc.

Cluster (also called **chunks** or **n-grams**):   A sequence of repeating words or phrases in a corpus; *one of the most* is a common four-word cluster in English. In AntConc, a cluster search starts with a word; the software returns the clusters where the specified word appears.

COCA | the Corpus of Contemporary American English: One billion words collected from 1990 to 2019, based on the architecture of the BNC. URL: www.english-corpora.org/coca.

Collocation | Collocate: Words that frequently occur together in a corpus collocate with each other; e.g. blond hair in English.

Concordance (lines):   A concordance is a sequence of lines of text from a corpus that shows the occurrence of a word or phrase in the middle; see Figure 4 for an example.

Concordancer: A tool for finding word patterns in texts (e.g. AntConc); a major use is to show concordance lines with the target word or phrase in the middle (see KWIC).

Corpus (plural **Corpora**):   A collection of written or spoken texts for analysis; usually in electronic format, selected to be representative of a language or part of a language.

Corpus linguistics: The study of language using corpora and associated tools such as concordancers.

Corpus search: The process of finding specific words or phrases in a corpus.

DDL | Data-Driven Learning: The use of the tools and techniques of corpus linguistics for learning and teaching language.

Frequency (absolute and **normalised)**:   The absolute frequency is the raw count of occurrences of a word in a corpus; as corpus sizes vary, the normalised frequency adjusts for corpus size, facilitating comparing frequencies across corpora (see PMW).

GenAI | Generative Artificial Intelligence: GenAI tools are likely to play a substantial role in language learning in coming years; however, unlike a corpus, the output is produced by machines, not humans, and is based on an opaque database.

Hands-on DDL | Hands-off DDL: Activities where language learners actively search a corpus to fulfil a task using software (hands-on) or prepared materials (hands-off).

Keyword: In corpus linguistics, a word or a phrase that occurs unusually often in one corpus compared to others.

KWIC | Key Word In Context: In a concordance software, the KWIC view shows target words centred with a few words of context either side; not to be confused with keyword.

Metadata: Information about the texts in a corpus, such as publication date, author, URL, etc.

N-gram: A sequence of any "n" words in a corpus (see Cluster).

Pattern: Recurring word combinations in language that reveal how lexical items and grammatical/syntactic relations collaborate to create meaning of common usage (as opposed to rules, which describe possible uses); see the *attack* group in Table 5.

PCs | Pedagogic corpora: Corpora such as SACODEYL/Backbone that are designed and collected to teach specific areas of an L2.

Phrase: In the context of a corpus search, a phrase is a string of words such as "just a thought" or "a thought".

PMW | per million words: A normalised frequency measure, useful when comparing corpora of substantially different sizes.

Range: In the context of a corpus search, range is the number of texts in a corpus where the search term can be found.

Register: A variety of language used in specific social situations; for example, face-to-face conversations or e-mails are different registers.

Representative corpora: Corpora that are designed to allow generalisations about genres or language varieties.

Sketch Engine: A corpus management tool for analysing word patterns, collocations and keywords. www.sketchengine.eu

Transcription | Transcript: Spoken language that is rendered as written text so that it can be queried using standard text-only corpus tools.

References

Ackermann, K., & Chen, Y.-H. (2013). Developing the academic collocation list (ACL): A corpus-driven and expert-judged approach. *Journal of English for Academic Purposes*, 12, 235–247. https://doi.org/10.1016/j.jeap.2013.08.002.

Adolphs, S., & Carter, R. (2003). 'And she's like it's terrible, like.' Spoken discourse, grammar and corpus analysis. *International Journal of English Studies*, 3(1), 45–56.

Amano, T., Ramírez-Castañeda, V., Berdejo-Espinola, V. et al. (2023). The manifold costs of being a non-native English speaker in science. *PLoS Biology*, 21(7), e3002184. https://doi.org/10.1371/journal.pbio.3002184.

Anthony, L. (2024). Addressing the challenges of Data-Driven learning through corpus tool design: In conversation with Laurence Anthony. In P. Crosthwaite (Ed.), *Corpora for language learning: Bridging the research-practice divide* (pp. 9–24). London: Routledge. https://doi.org/10.4324/9781003413301-2.

Baker, P. (2009). The BE06 Corpus of British English and recent language change. *International Journal of Corpus Linguistics*, 14(3), 312–337. https://doi.org/10.1075/ijcl.14.3.02bak.

Ballance, O. J. (2017). Pedagogical models of concordance use: Correlations between concordance user preferences. *Computer Assisted Language Learning*, 30(3–4), 259–283. https://doi.org/10.1080/09588221.2017.1307228.

Biber, D., Johansson, S., Leech, G., Conrad, S., & Finegan, E. (1999). *Longman grammar of spoken and written English*. London: Pearson.

Boulton, A. (2015). Applying Data-Driven learning to the web. In A. Leńko-Szymańska & A. Boulton (Eds.), *Multiple affordances of language corpora for Data-Driven learning* (pp. 267–295). Amsterdam: John Benjamins. https://doi.org/10.1075/scl.69.13bou.

Boulton, A. (2021). Research in Data-Driven learning. In P. Pérez-Paredes & G. Mark (Eds.), *Beyond the concordance: Corpora in language education* (pp. 9–34). Amsterdam: John Benjamins. https://doi.org/10.1075/scl.102.01bou.

Boulton, A. (2024). Corpus à volonté: À l'écoute des étudiants. *Humanités, Didactiques, Recherches*, 4, 117–136.

Boulton, A., & Cobb, T. (2017). Corpus use in language learning: A meta-analysis. *Language Learning*, 67(2), 348–393. https://doi.org/10.1111/lang.12224.

Boulton, A., & Pérez-Paredes, P. (2024). Data-Driven learning: Pedagogy and technology. In R. Hampel & U. Stickler (Eds.), *Bloomsbury handbook of language learning and technology* (pp. 212–225). London: Bloomsbury.

Boulton, A., & Vyatkina, N. (2021). Thirty years of Data-Driven learning: Taking stock and charting new directions. *Language Learning & Technology*, 25(3), 66–89. https://doi.org/10125/73450.

Boulton, A., & Vyatkina, N. (2024). Expanding methodological approaches in DDL research. *TESOL Quarterly*, 58(3), 1193–1204. https://doi.org/10.1002/tesq.3269.

Boulton, A., Vyatkina, N., & Cobb, T. (in press). Classroom applications of corpus analysis. In D. Biber & R. Reppen (Eds.), *Cambridge handbook of English corpus linguistics* (2nd ed.). Cambridge University Press.

Braun, S. (2005). From pedagogically relevant corpora to authentic language learning contents. *ReCALL*, 17(1), 47–64. https://doi.org/10.1017/S0958344005000510.

Braun, S. (2006). ELISA: A pedagogically enriched corpus for language learning purposes. In S. Braun, K. Kohn, & J. Mukherjee (Eds.), *Corpus technology and language pedagogy: New resources, new tools, new methods* (pp. 25–47). Frankfurt: Peter Lang.

Braun, S. (2007). Integrating corpus work into secondary education: From Data-Driven learning to needs-driven corpora. *ReCALL*, 19(3), 307–328. https://doi.org/10.1017/S0958344007000535.

Brezina, V., & Platt, W. (2024). #LancsBox X [software]. Lancaster University. http://lancsbox.lancs.ac.uk.

Carter, R., & McCarthy, M. (1995). Grammar and the spoken language. *Applied Linguistics*, 16, 141–158. https://doi.org/10.1093/applin/16.2.141.

Charles, M. (2018). Corpus-assisted editing for doctoral students: More than just concordancing. *Journal of English for Academic Purposes*, 36, 15–25. https://doi.org/10.1016/j.jeap.2018.08.003.

Charles, M. (2022). The gap between intentions and reality: Reasons for EAP writers' non-use of corpora. *Applied Corpus Linguistics*, 2(3), 100032. https://doi.org/10.1016/j.acorp.2022.100032.

Charles, M., & Frankenberg-Garcia, A. (Eds.) (2021). *Corpora in EAP/ESP writing: Preparation, exploitation and analysis*. London: Routledge. https://doi.org/10.4324/9781003001966.

Charles, M., & Hadley, G. (2022). Autonomous corpus use by graduate students: A long-term trend study (2009–2017). *Journal of English for Academic Purposes*, 56, 101095. https://doi.org/10.1016/j.jeap.2022.101095.

Chen, H.-J. H., Lai, S.-L., Lee, K.-Y., & Yang, C. T.-Y. (2023). Developing and evaluating an academic collocations and phrases search engine for academic writers. *Computer Assisted Language Learning*, 36(4), 641–668. https://doi.org/10.1080/09588221.2021.1937229.

Chen, H. C., & Tian, J. X. (2022). Developing and evaluating a flipped corpus-aided English pronunciation teaching approach for pre-service teachers in Hong Kong. *Interactive Learning Environments*, 30(10), 1918–1931. https://doi.org/10.1080/10494820.2020.1753217.

Cobb, T. (2024). *Compleat Lexical Tutor* v.8.5. Accessed 15 July 2024 at www.lextutor.ca/.

Cobb, T. (forthcoming). Word lists in Data-Driven learning. In A. Boulton & N. Vyatkina (Eds.), *Data-Driven and corpus-based CALL – Encyclopedia of computer-assisted language learning*. Basingstoke: Palgrave Macmillan.

Cobb, T., Nation, P., & McQuillan, T. (2016). Discussion forum. *Reading in a Foreign Language*, 28(2), 299–318. https://nflrc.hawaii.edu/rfl/collection/col_10125_68076.

Coxhead, A. (2000). A new academic word list. *TESOL Quarterly*, 34(2), 213–238.

Crosthwaite, P. (Ed.) (2019). *Data-Driven learning for the next generation: Corpora and DDL for pre-tertiary learners*. Abingdon: Routledge.

Crosthwaite, P., & Baisa, V. (2023). Generative AI and the end of corpus-assisted Data-Driven learning? Not so fast! *Applied Corpus Linguistics*, 3(3), 100066. https://doi.org/10.1016/j.acorp.2023.100066.

Crosthwaite, P., & Baisa, V. (2024). Introducing CorpusMate: A user-friendly corpus tool for disciplinary Data-Driven Learning. International Journal of Corpus Linguistics, 29(4), 595–610, advance access. https://doi.org/10.1075/ijcl.23056.cro.

Curry, M. J., & Lillis, T. (2024). Multilingualism in academic writing for publication: Putting English in its place. *Language Teaching*, 57(1), 87–100. https://doi.org/10.1017/S0261444822000040.

Curry, N., Love, R., & Goodman, O. (2022). Adverbs on the move: Investigating publisher application of corpus research on recent language change to ELT coursebook development. *Corpora*, 17(1), 1–38. https://doi.org/10.3366/cor.2022.0233.

Davies, M. (2009). The 385+ million word Corpus of Contemporary American English (1990–2008+): Design, architecture, and linguistic insights. *International Journal of Corpus Linguistics*, 14(2), 159–188. https://doi.org/10.1075/ijcl.14.2.02dav.

Dong, J., Zhao, Y., & Buckingham, L. (2023). Charting the landscape of Data-Driven learning using a bibliometric analysis. *ReCALL*, 35(3), 339–355. https://doi.org/10.1017/S0958344022000222.

Flowerdew, L. (2009). Applying corpus linguistics to pedagogy: A critical evaluation. *International Journal of Corpus Linguistics*, 14(3), 393–417. https://doi.org/10.1075/ijcl.14.3.05flo.

Flowerdew J. (2024). Data-Driven learning: From Collins Cobuild dictionary to ChatGPT. *Language Teaching*, advance access. https://doi.org/10.1017/S0261444824000144.

Frankenberg-Garcia, A., Lew, R., Roberts, J. C., Rees, G. P., & Sharma, N. (2019). Developing a writing assistant to help EAP writers with collocations in real time. *ReCALL*, 31(1), 23–39. https://doi.org/10.1017/S0958344018000150.

Frankenberg-Garcia, A., Tavares Pinto, P., Bocorny, A., & Sarmento, S. (2022). Corpus-aided EAP writing workshops to support international scholarly publication. *Applied Corpus Linguistics*, 2(3), 100029. https://doi.org/10.1016/j.acorp.2022.100029.

Friginal, E., & Roberts, J. (2022). Corpora for materials design. In R. R. Jablonkai & E. Csomay (Eds.), *The Routledge handbook of corpora and English language teaching and learning* (pp. 131–146). London: Routledge. https://doi.org/10.4324/9781003002901-11.

Fu, J. S., & Yang, S.-H. (2019). Exploring how YouGlish facilitates EFL learners' speaking competence. *Educational Technology & Society*, 22(4), 47–58. www.j-ets.net/collection/published-issues/22_4.

Gablasova, D., & Bottini, R. (2022). Spoken learner corpora for language teaching. In R. R. Jablonkai & E. Csomay (Eds.), *The Routledge handbook of corpora and English language teaching and learning* (pp. 296–310). London: Routledge. https://doi.org/10.4324/9781003002901-24.

Gardner, D., & Davies, M. (2014). A new academic vocabulary list. *Applied Linguistics*, 35(3), 305–327. https://doi.org/10.1093/applin/amt015.

Gaskell, D., & Cobb, T. (2004). Can learners use concordance feedback for writing errors? *System*, 32(3), 301–319. https://doi.org/10.1016/j.system.2004.04.001.

Gatto, M. (2019). Query complexity and query refinement: Using web search from a corpus perspective with digital natives. In P. Crosthwaite (Ed.), *Data-Driven learning for the next generation* (pp. 106–130). London: Routledge. https://doi.org/10.4324/9780429425899-7.

Gee, J., & Hayes, E. (2011). *Language and learning in the digital age*. London: Routledge.

Götz, S., & Mukherjee, J. (Eds.) (2019). *Learner corpora and language teaching*. Amsterdam: John Benjamins. https://doi.org/10.1075/scl.92.

Hadley, G., & Charles, M. (2017). Enhancing extensive reading with Data-Driven learning. *Language Learning & Technology*, 21(3), 131–152. https://doi.org/10125/44624.

Han, S., & Shin, J.-A. (2017). Teaching Google search techniques in an L2 academic writing context. *Language Learning & Technology*, 21(3), 172–194. https://doi.org/10125/44626.

Hoffstaedter, P., & Kohn, K. (2009). Real language and relevant language learning activities: Insights from the SACODEYL project. In Stinshoff, R. (Ed), *The workings of the anglosphere: Contributions to the study of British and US-American cultures* (pp. 291–303). Trier: WVT.

Hunston, S. (2019). Patterns, constructions, and applied linguistics. *International Journal of Corpus Linguistics*, 24(3), 324–353. https://doi .org/10.1075/ijcl.00015.hun.

Hunston, S., & Francis, G. (2000). *Pattern grammar: A corpus-driven approach to the lexical grammar of English*. Amsterdam: John Benjamins. https://doi .org/10.1075/scl.4.

Hyland, K. (2016). Academic publishing and the myth of linguistic injustice. *Journal of Second Language Writing*, 31, 58–69. http://dx.doi.org/10.1016/j .jslw.2016.01.005.

Johns, T. (1986). Micro-Concord: A language learner's research tool. *System*, 14(2), 151–162. https://doi.org/10.1016/0346-251X(86)90004-7.

Johns, T. (1990). From printout to handout: Grammar and vocabulary teaching in the context of Data-Driven learning. *CALL Austria*, 10, 14–34.

Johns, T. (2002). Data-Driven learning: The perpetual challenge. In B. Kettemann & G. Marko (Eds.), *Teaching and learning by doing corpus analysis* (pp. 107–117). Amsterdam: Rodopi. https://doi.org/10.1163/ 9789004334236_010.

Johns, T., Lee, H., & Wang, L. (2008). Integrating corpus-based CALL programs and teaching English through children's literature. *Computer Assisted Language Learning*, 21(5), 483–506. https://doi.org/10.1080/09588220802448006.

Jordan, G., & Long, M. (2023). *English language teaching now and how it could be*. Newcastle: Cambridge Scholars.

Kang, E. Y., Sok, S., & Han, Z. (2019). Thirty-five years of ISLA on form-focused instruction: A meta-analysis. *Language Teaching Research*, 23(4), 428–453. https://doi.org/10.1177/1362168818776671.

Kic-Drgas, J., Seferoğlu, G., Kılıçkaya, F., & Pereira, R. (2023). Polish, Portuguese, and Turkish EFL teachers' perceptions on the use of OER language processing technologies in MALL: A replication study. *ReCALL*, 35(2), 143–159. https://doi.org/10.1017/S0958344023000058.

Kilgarriff, A., Baisa, V., Bušta, J. et al. (2014). The sketch engine: Ten years on. *Lexicography*, 1(1), 7–36. https://doi.org/10.1007/s40607-014-0009-9.

Lai, S.-L., Chang, J., Lee, K.-L., & Huang, W.-C. (2022). Linggle 2.0: A collocation retrieval system with quality example sentences. In B. Arnbjörnsdóttir, B. Bédi, L. Bradley et al. (Eds.), *Intelligent CALL, granular systems, and learner data* (pp. 234–239). Dublin: Research-publishing.net. https://doi.org/10.14705/rpnet.2022.61.1464.

Laufer, B., & Cobb, T. (2020). How much knowledge of derived words is needed for reading? *Applied Linguistics*, 41(6), 971–998. https://doi.org/10.1093/applin/amz051.

Lee, H., Warschauer, M., & Lee, J. H. (2019). The effects of corpus use on second language vocabulary learning: A multi-level analysis. *Applied Linguistics*, 40(5), 721–753. https://doi.org/10.1093/applin/amy012.

Le Foll, E. (Ed.). (2021). Creating corpus-informed materials for the English as a foreign language classroom: A step-by-step guide for (trainee) teachers using online resources. [Open Educational Resource.] Zenodo. https://doi.org/10.5281/zenodo.4992504.

Leńko-Szymańska, A., & Boulton, A. (Eds.). (2015). *Multiple affordances of language corpora for Data-Driven learning*. Amsterdam: John Benjamins. https://doi.org/10.1075/scl.69.

Lin, P. (2023). ChatGPT: Friend or foe (to corpus linguists)? *Applied Corpus Linguistics*, 3(3), 100065. https://doi.org/10.1016/j.acorp.2023.100065.

McCarthy, M., McEnery, T., Mark, G., & Pérez-Paredes, P. (2021). Looking back on 25 years of TaLC: In conversation with Profs Mike McCarthy and Tony McEnery. In P. Pérez-Paredes & G. Mark (Eds.), *Beyond concordance lines: Applications of corpora in language education* (pp. 57–74). Amsterdam: John Benjamins. https://doi.org/10.1075/scl.102.03mcc.

McEnery, T., & Brezina, V. (2022). *Fundamental principles of corpus linguistics*. Cambridge: Cambridge University Press. https://doi.org/10.1017/9781107110625.

McEnery, T., & Wilson, A. (1997). Teaching and language corpora (TALC). *ReCALL*, 9(1), 5–14. https://doi.org/10.1017/S0958344000004572.

Meunier, F. (2019). A case for constructive alignment in DDL: Rethinking outcomes, practices, and assessment in (Data-Driven) language learning. In P. Crosthwaite (Ed.), *Data-Driven learning for the next generation* (pp. 13–30). London: Routledge. https://doi.org/10.4324/9780429425899-2.

Miras, G., Boulton, A., Kübler, N., & Narcy-Combes, J.-P. (2018). Association française de linguistique appliquée (AFLA). *European Journal of Applied Linguistics*, 6(2), 315–326. https://doi.org/10.1515/eujal-2018-0004.

Mishan, F. (2004). Authenticating corpora for language learning: A problem and its resolution. *ELT Journal*, 58(3), 219–227. https://doi.org/10.1093/elt/58.3.219.

Mizumoto, A. (2023). Data-Driven learning meets generative AI: Introducing the framework of metacognitive resource use. *Applied Corpus Linguistics*, 3(3), 100074. https://doi.org/10.1016/j.acorp.2023.100074.

Nergis, A. (2021). Can explicit instruction of formulaic sequences enhance L2 oral fluency? *Lingua*, 255, 103072. https://doi.org/10.1016/j.lingua.2021.103072.

Ngo, T. T.-N., & Chen, H. H.-J. (2024). The effectiveness of corpus use in ESL/EFL writing: A meta-analysis. *Language Teaching Research*, advance access. https://doi.org/10.1177/13621688241260183.

O'Keeffe, A. (2021). Data-Driven learning, theories of learning and second language acquisition. In P. Pérez-Paredes & G. Mark (Eds.), *Beyond concordance lines: Corpora in language education* (pp. 35–56). Amsterdam: John Benjamins. https://doi.org/10.1075/scl.102.02oke.

Pérez-Paredes, P. (2019). The pedagogic advantage of teenage corpora for secondary school learners. In P. Crosthwaite (Ed.), *Data-Driven learning for the next generation: Corpora and DDL for pre-tertiary learners* (pp. 67–87). London: Routledge. https://doi.org/10.4324/9780429425899-5.

Pérez-Paredes, P. (2020). *Corpus linguistics for education: A guide for research*. London: Routledge. https://doi.org/10.4324/9780429243615.

Pérez-Paredes, P. (2022). A systematic review of the uses and spread of corpora and Data-Driven learning in CALL research during 2011–2015. *Computer Assisted Language Learning*, 35(1–2), 36–61. https://doi.org/10.1080/09588221.2019.1667832.

Pérez-Paredes, P. (2024). Data-Driven learning in informal contexts? Embracing broad Data-Driven learning (BDDL) research. In P. Crosthwaite (Ed.), *Corpora for language learning: Bridging the research-practice divide* (pp. 211–226). London: Routledge.

Pérez-Paredes, P., & Abad, M. (in press). Integrating language teachers' voices in the design and exploitation of Spanish corpora in the UK. In H. Tyne & S. Spina (Eds.), *Applying corpora in teaching and learning Romance languages*. Amsterdam: John Benjamins.

Pérez-Paredes, P., Aguado-Jiménez, P., & Ordoñana Guillamón, C. (2025). Using corpus data to facilitate engagement with mass media texts. In V. Viana (Ed.), *International perspectives on corpus applications in ELT*. Basingstoke: Palgrave.

Pérez-Paredes, P., & Boulton, A. (2024). *A list of tools and resources that facilitate Data-Driven learning (DDL)*. University of York: IRIS Database. https://doi.org/10.48316/DgLhT-C33sa.

Pérez-Paredes, P., & Chambers, A. (in press). Corpora and the learning and teaching of romance languages. In H. Tyne & S. Spina (Eds.), *Applying corpora in teaching and learning Romance languages*. Amsterdam: John Benjamins.

Pérez-Paredes, P., & Mark, G. (Eds.) (2021). *Beyond concordance lines: Applications of corpora in language education*. Amsterdam: John Benjamins. https://doi.org/10.1075/scl.102.

Pérez-Paredes, P., Ordoñana, C., & Aguado, P. (2018). Language teachers' perceptions on the use of OER language processing technologies in MALL.

Computer Assisted Language Learning, 31(5–6), 522–545. https://doi.org/10.1080/09588221.2017.1418754.

Pérez-Paredes, P., Sánchez-Tornel, M., & Alcaraz Calero, J. M. (2012). Learners' search patterns during corpus-based focus-on-form activities. *International Journal of Corpus Linguistics*, 17, 483–516. https://doi.org/10.1075/ijcl.17.4.02par.

Plonsky, L., & Oswald, F. L. (2014). How big is 'big'? Interpreting effect sizes in L2 research. *Language Learning*, 64, 878–912. https://doi.org/10.1111/lang.12079.

Schmidt, R. (1990). The role of consciousness in second language learning. *Applied Linguistics*, 11(2), 129–158. https://doi.org/10.1093/applin/11.2.129.

Simpson-Vlach, R., & Ellis, N. (2010). An academic formulas list: New methods in phraseology research. *Applied Linguistics*, 31(4), 487–512. https://doi.org/10.1093/applin/amp058.

Sinclair, J. (1991). *Corpus, concordance, collocation.* Oxford: Oxford University Press.

Sinclair, J. (2003). *Reading concordances: An introduction.* Harlow: Longman.

Smith, S. (2020). DIY corpora for accounting & finance vocabulary learning. *English for Specific Purposes*, 57, 1–12. https://doi.org/10.1016/j.esp.2019.08.002.

Spivey, M. (2023). Data-Driven learning and young learners: Perceptions and attitudes of Japanese elementary school students toward EFL corpus-based activities. *JALT CALL Journal*, 19(3), 394–416. https://doi.org/10.29140/jaltcall.v19n3.1014.

Swales, J., & Feak, C. (2010). *Academic writing for graduate students* (3rd ed.). Ann Arbor: University of Michigan Press. https://doi.org/10.3998/mpub.2173936.

Szudarski, P. (2019). Effects of Data-Driven learning on enhancing the phraseological knowledge of secondary school learners of L2 English. In P. Crosthwaite (Ed.), *Data-Driven learning for the next generation* (pp. 133–149). London: Routledge. https://doi.org/10.4324/9780429425899-8.

Szudarski, P. (2022). Corpora and teaching vocabulary and phraseology. In R. R. Jablonkai & E. Csomay (Eds.), *The Routledge handbook of corpora and English language teaching and learning* (pp. 41–55). London: Routledge. https://doi.org/10.4324/9781003002901-5.

Szudarski, P., & Carter, R. (2016). The role of input flood and input enhancement in EFL learners' acquisition of collocations. *International Journal of Applied Linguistics*, 26(2), 245–265. https://doi.org/10.1111/ijal.12092.

Tomasello, M. (2003). *Constructing a language: A usage-based theory of language acquisition*. Cambridge MA: Harvard University Press.

Tschichold, C., Boulton, A., & Pérez-Paredes, P. (2024). Interpreting the review process in applied linguistics research. In S.-W. Chong (Ed.), *Developing feedback literacy for academic journal peer review* (pp. 41–59). London: Routledge.

Tyne, H., & S. Spina (Eds.) (in press). *Applying corpora in teaching and learning Romance languages*. Amsterdam: John Benjamins.

Ueno, S., & Takeuchi, O. (2023). Effective corpus use in second language learning: A meta-analytic approach. *Applied Corpus Linguistics*, 3(3), 100076. https://doi.org/10.1016/j.acorp.2023.100076.

Viana, V. (2022). *Teaching English with corpora: A resource book*. London: Routledge. https://doi.org/10.4324/b22833.

Vyatkina, N. (2020). Corpora as open educational resources for language teaching. *Foreign Language Annals*, 53(2), 359–370. https://doi.org/10.1111/flan.12464.

Widmann, J., Kohn, K., & Ziai, R. (2011). The SACODEYL search tool: Exploiting corpora for language learning purposes. In A. Frankenberg-Garcia, L. Flowerdew, & G. Aston (Eds.), *New trends in corpora and language learning* (pp. 167–178). London: Continuum.

Acknowledgements

We first need to thank our colleagues and co-authors in previous publications who have tremendously informed our practice and understanding of the approach discussed here, the tools and techniques, theories and methodologies. Thanks to the Editors and the anonymous Reviewers for their suggestions, as well as to Jarvis Looi and Jiaqi Guo for reading our draft and providing great feedback. Thank you also to our students over the years. Our thanks too to Laurence Anthony, Mark Davies and the Sketch Engine team for their dedication to providing tools for DDL, their support and reactivity to us and all the DDL community. Thanks to all who gave permission to use screenshots from their software and websites.

Cambridge Elements

Language Teaching

Heath Rose
University of Oxford

Heath Rose is Professor of Applied Linguistics at the University of Oxford and Deputy Director (People) of the Department of Education. Before moving into academia, Heath worked as a language teacher in Australia and Japan in both school and university contexts. He is author of numerous books, such as *Introducing Global Englishes, The Japanese Writing System, Data Collection Research Methods in Applied Linguistics,* and *Global Englishes for Language Teaching.*

Jim McKinley
University College London

Jim McKinley is Professor of Applied Linguistics at IOE Faculty of Education and Society, University College London. He has taught in higher education in the UK, Japan, Australia, and Uganda, as well as US schools. His research targets implications of globalization for L2 writing, language education, and higher education studies, particularly the teaching-research nexus and English medium instruction. Jim is co-author and co-editor of several books on research methods in applied linguistics. He is an Editor-in-Chief of the journal System.

Advisory Board

Gary Barkhuizen, *University of Auckland*
Marta Gonzalez-Lloret, *University of Hawaii*
Li Wei, *UCL Institute of Education*
Victoria Murphy, *University of Oxford*
Brian Paltridge, *University of Sydney*
Diane Pecorari, *Leeds University*
Christa Van der Walt, *Stellenbosch University*
Yongyan Zheng, *Fudan University*

About the Series

This Elements series aims to close the gap between researchers and practitioners by allying research with language teaching practices, in its exploration of research informed teaching, and teaching-informed research. The series builds upon a rich history of pedagogical research in its exploration of new insights within the field of language teaching.

For EU product safety concerns, contact us at Calle de José Abascal, 56–1°,
28003 Madrid, Spain or eugpsr@cambridge.org.

www.ingramcontent.com/pod-product-compliance
Ingram Content Group UK Ltd.
Pitfield, Milton Keynes, MK11 3LW, UK
UKHW021459220625
459949UK00018B/500